TAROT AND ASTROLOGY

TAROT
AND
ASTROLOGY
The Pursuit of Destiny

Muriel Bruce Hasbrouck

Destiny Books
Rochester, Vermont

Destiny Books
One Park Street
Rochester, Vermont 05767
www.DestinyBooks.com

Copyright © 1941, 1969, 1976, 1986, 1989, 1996 by Muriel Bruce Hasbrouck

LIBRARY OF CONGRESS CATALOGING-IN-PUBLICATION DATA

Hasbrouck, Muriel Bruce.
    [Pursuit of destiny]
    Tarot and astrology : the pursuit of destiny / by Muriel Bruce Hasbrouck.
        p. cm.
    Previously published: 1986.
    ISBN 978-0-89281-121-2
    1. Astrology. 2. Zodiac. 3. Tarot. I. Title.
[BF1711.H27 1996]
133.5–dc20   96–13897
                                                CIP

Printed and bound in the United States

20 19 18 17 16 15 14 13 12 11

To

PULCH, PERDURABO, and PAUL,
*who started me, guided me,
and disciplined me, in the
pursuit of my own destiny.*

THE TEN DAY CYCLES
as they occur during
THE FOUR WAVES OF THE SOLAR YEAR

with their Basic Qualities, Potentials, and Frequencies
indicated by shading, numbers, and symbols

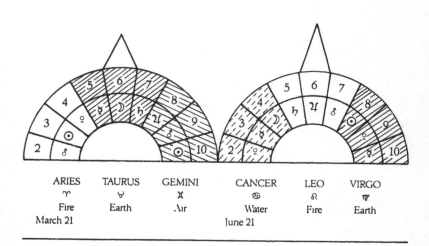

ARIES	TAURUS	GEMINI	CANCER	LEO	VIRGO
♈	♉	♊	♋	♌	♍
Fire	Earth	Air	Water	Fire	Earth
March 21			June 21		

THE FOUR BASIC QUALITIES

☐	Fire
▨	Water
▨	Earth
▧	Air

THE SEVEN PLANETARY SYMBOLS

⊙ Sun

♀ Venus	☿ Mercury	☽ Moon
♄ Saturn	♃ Jupiter	♂ Mars

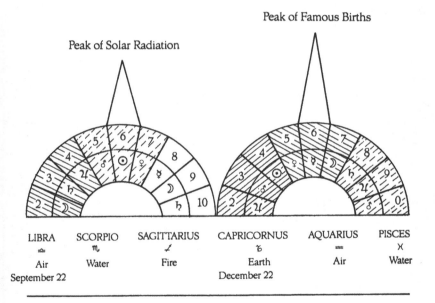

Peak of Famous Births

Peak of Solar Radiation

LIBRA	SCORPIO	SAGITTARIUS	CAPRICORNUS	AQUARIUS	PISCES
♎	♏	♐	♑	♒	♓
Air	Water	Fire	Earth	Air	Water
September 22			December 22		

'Every individuality is indefinitely perfectible.'

CONTENTS

— the inferiority complex — the individual standard — famous people's behaviour — dictators, rulers and leaders — the individual in history — family and personal relationships.

FOREWORD

When a famous man was asked, the other day, to name the most important event in his life, he answered — 'Being born!'

No argument there. But the essential, physical fact of birth is only the beginning of its importance. For many centuries — so many that the concept cannot be put aside — there has been a universal belief that the *time* of birth, because it can be interpreted as an indication of the meaningful identity of the individual, is of the utmost importance in itself. This persistent, undying belief has given rise to systems of thought at the highest levels of harmonic order. These systems are always based on a simple structure of what can only be called cosmological humanism, linking visible celestial mechanisms with everyday life on earth.

When we originated the formula presented in this book, correlating for the first time the ancient beliefs with modern psychology and science, its consistent accuracy in personality study met with puzzled skepticism, especially from the scientific world. But during the last forty-five years, this scientific stiffness has been forced, by developments within its own research and discovery, to change, relax, and even (now and then) to question and inquire.

Also, since the end of World War Two, a cyclic wave of discontent, particularly, but not exclusively, affecting the young, has swept over the world. It is suddenly apparent that in the eternal quest for a meaningful identity, the old religions and philosophies have completely broken down. This world-wide shift in mass psychology has brought about a resurgence of popularity for all forms of 'occultism' with top billing given to astrology. This recent outburst naturally carries a coating of superstitious barnacles, the accretion of centuries. But in the clear light of today's realities, there could be no development more natural and relevant — and more encouraging — than the current epidemic of a need to solve, by any available means, the central problem of every individual. *Who am I? What is it all about?*

This turn of direction in mass psychology is undoubtedly due to the fact that scientific thinking, since the advent of the Space Age, has not been confined to academic ivory towers. It has touched every area of life, bringing a universal ability to *see* and *hear* far (and fast) beyond our earlier limitations. How can modern youth, or their elders, be expected to conform with outworn unrealities when, with every day that passes, new and tangible realities bombard their eyes and ears and stir their minds to action? Man has suddenly reawakened to the fact that he is part of a vast cosmos; he is not a mere speck of dust on a chunk of matter revolving round the sun. And, with this new dawn of cosmic realization, where better can the questing mind find answers to personal problems than within the age-old beliefs that lie at the heart of man's instinctive recognition of the importance of a birthdate? Especially now, when the recognition has been combined, as in this book, with the findings of modern science and psychology.

Few people are aware — while fortune-tellers thrive, and computers are called in to sort out the confusion between zodiac signs, planets, and birthdates — that today modern science is rediscovering that people, and all other 'living systems' are actually part of a *unified field of energy*, considered to be of solar origin, within which the entire world functions naturally and inevitably, and which changes with time. What reasonable connection, however, can exist between this modern field-force concept and the importance of a birthday?

Being born is a catastrophic event. You, the new arrival, are thrust into a strange, unfriendly element. Why should the timing of this event be so important that it can condition the whole course of your life? A simple correlation of biological fact with field theory suggests an answer. If the physical body, in all its ordered complexity, can spring from an infinitesimal nucleus, the psychological structure of the individual can also have a nucleus. Is it not reasonable to imply that at the 'moment of time' when the individual becomes a part of the earth's electromagnetic field *with the drawing of the first breath*, the newborn organism receives a 'charge' from the field, a psychological nucleus, image of the personality that will develop through life?

Many centuries ago, Chinese philosophy (Tao) put it this way: 'At the time of birth, the conscious spirit draws in the power of the air, and thus becomes the dwelling of the newborn.' Closer to our own time, the great psychologist, Carl Gustav Jung, expressed this concept with more clarity. After a lifetime of study devoted to science and philosophy pertaining to human personality, he wrote: 'That which is born or done in this moment of time has the *qualities* of this moment of time.'

But what are the qualities of time? Where can they be located? How can they be measured and appraised, relative to the 'moment of time' in which the birth takes place?

A quest for answers to these questions was undertaken by this writer many years ago, joined, in the early thirties, by a skeptical, but equally curious husband. He, too, had been searching for answers to related questions — what, if any, are the forces that lie behind the changing trends in world affairs? As both quests concerned *people* — why they behave, and misbehave, the way they do — the two blended easily into one.

We began by carrying through what I had begun earlier, a critical, exhaustive examination of every system and method ever used in connection with astrology. It was soon obvious that the answers we sought could not be found in the conglomerate confusions of that subject, but the concept *behind* the confusion was not to be dismissed; there was too much evidence in its favour. Kepler, greatest of astronomers, insisted to the day he died that somewhere, in what he called the astrological rubbish heap, there was a hidden treasure, a 'pearl' to be discovered. It was by carrying our search deeply into history, mythology, and modern physics, that we found what we were looking for.

As often happens in research, the answer came from an unexpected source. Just as we were about to give up in despair, we came upon what could only be a structural system, or pattern, of 'the qualities of time'. Accurately calculated, correlated, and defined, this answer was discovered in the ancient, colourful, supposedly mysterious pack of cards known as the Tarot.

INTRODUCTION

One of the most persistent conceptions in all the history of human thinking has been the idea that there is a definable relationship between the birthdate and the destiny of a human individual. This is a very old idea; it crops up in the records of every known civilization and culture. It possesses an irrevocable charm, an everlasting allure — which may be one of the reasons why it has been frowned upon throughout the Christian era, first by ecclesiastical and later by scientific authority. Until recently, the idea of TIME as being in any sense a conditioning factor in human life has been regarded as a fantastic notion, unfit for intelligent consideration.

Today, however, with the development of modern physics, in which the theories of Relativity and Quanta are opening new vistas into time and space, the scholastic viewpoint is noticeably changing. Many scientists are studying quite seriously the possibility of a connection between man and his cosmic environment, even to the point of analyzing seasonal influences, according to birthdate, on individual potentialities. Science, while remaining skeptical, is becoming, in certain areas, more open-minded on these questions, which is one of the things that has made possible this new presentation of the ancient and controversial subject of birthdates and destiny.

With any new presentation of an old subject, prejudices which were attached to the older hypothesis are apt to create, at first view, a subconscious hurdle of skepticism on the part of the reader. It seems that in this case the hurdle can be taken with some confidence, because of the evident convergence of the ancient and modern hypotheses. The particular point of convergence — where ancient theories and modern knowledge meet and begin to agree — is the modern scientific interest in the Sun and its importance to the welfare and progress of mankind. Fortunes are being poured out in the search for exact information relating to the influence of the Sun on human life, such influence being, in the words of Dr Harlan T. Stetson, 'speculative but not at all impossible.'

While science is focusing its instruments on solar radiation, a corresponding phenomenon has appeared in the practical world. From Wall Street to the inner sanctums of great research institutes — in business, economics, and government — the subject of 'time cycles' is being discussed, studied, and developed. Modern thought, it seems, is turning toward the theory held in ancient and medieval days that the course of time is not a mere abstraction, but that it is a process almost tangible in its concrete significance — in short, that time is a factor which must be reckoned with in the understanding and conduct of human life. Physicists have even coined a new name for it: they call it *the space-time continuum*.

This book contains the initial report of an independent research in the field of time cycles as related to birthdate conditioning. It has been said that the two best qualifications for a research worker are curiosity and ignorance, and in relation to my chosen subject, I think I may lay claim to a bit more than the average curiosity, plus my fair share of the general ignorance in the matter. My original interest in the idea of time-conditioning arose out of a writer's natural desire to understand people as individuals. I started out to look for a basis on which to analyze personalities — their similarities, their differences, and their relationships with each other. After failing to find any such basis in the modern, orthodox sciences, such as biology and psychology, the ancient, unorthodox theories of birthdate and time-conditioning attracted my attention as a possible source of information.

Because of the scarcity of authentic records, any research in the field of ancient and medieval knowledge is a tough assignment, as other investigators have found before me. Two things impelled me to continue the work in the face of contradictory evidence, illogical and disappointing results, and the ridicule of almost everybody I knew. One was the fascination of the idea itself — the idea of a definable correlation between human destiny and the natural course of time. The other was a conviction that if so many people had accepted, and used, the idea of birthdate and time-conditioning for uncounted centuries, there must be something in it.

My persistence was finally rewarded in the summer of 1932, when I came upon a document which provided the first clue to an orderly, practical pattern of time. This document was a detailed description of the ancient and mysterious pack of cards known as the TAROT, which was probably the original form and precursor of modern standard playing cards. The clue lay in the odd fact that every card in the ancient pack, as described in the document, was directly linked in one way or another with a specific period of time within the solar year. Also, the descriptions of the spot cards were so expressed that it seemed they should apply to individual psychology, and they — the spot cards — covered the entire solar year in a series of ten-degree cycles, approximately ten days in length.

This suggested to me the possibility that the original birthdate-conditioning formula — used by the scientists of antiquity with the evident approval of kings, priests, and scholars, as well as of the populace — had been based upon a recurrent *ten-day cycle* rather than upon the generally accepted thirty-day zodiacal divisions of the solar year.

In addition to the timing system, and the psychological descriptions, this document provided a series of symbols — mythological, alchemical, and kabalistic — which lent themselves to analysis and enabled me to construct, for the first time in the course of my research, an orderly and logical pattern of changes in the field of the solar year. These changes, it seemed, *might* induce a series of corresponding responses in human behaviour, and thereby offer the basis for a birthdate-conditioning formula.

When put to the test with actual personalities and birthdates, the psychological pattern of the ten-day cycles proved itself, from the first, to be both accurate and useful. In nearly nine years of testing and correlating — carried out from a consistently skeptical viewpoint — the ten-day cycle hypothesis has grown into a formula of time-conditioning that cannot be dismissed as either coincidence or fantasy. Here, my thanks are due to the many people who lent themselves and their birthdays for study and analysis during the course of the research, and to my husband, who has been actively

— and indispensably — associated with the work from its inception.

As with many another formula, this one is not easily explained. But here we are reminded of the professor's statement about the famous mathematical formula $e^{i\pi}+1=0$: 'We cannot understand it and we don't know what it means, but we have proved it, and therefore we know it must be the truth.'

We know two things about the Ten-Day Cycle Formula. First, from the nature of its sources, we know it has been in existence for many centuries, and that it must have been worked out empirically, at some time, with considerable and meticulous labour. Second, from the results of practical experiment, we know that it works. Because of this — because it has proved to be of real value to many individuals who were puzzled about themselves, their families, friends, and enemies — the Formula is here set forth in considerable detail. Included, for those who may be interested, is the story of its history and background, revealing the strange and provocative link between the structure of the solar year and the structure — as well as the possible origin — of the pack of cards.

As it is here presented, the Ten-Day Cycle Formula can be used as a tentative guidepost in the pursuit of destiny by everyone who has a birthday. For those who need no guideposts, it is my hope that the Formula will serve as a steppingstone, or even as an escape, from the chaotic conceptions of life and humanity forced upon us by appearances, toward a feeling of confidence in what Einstein so beautifully called '*the inner harmony* of *the world*'.

For the accomplishment of the tasks of human reconstruction that lie before us in the next few decades, we are going to need a restoration of our faith in destiny, as something worth pursuing. Perhaps this reshaping of an ancient faith, adapted to modern form and expression, may provide some part of the mental and spiritual mechanism of the future.

M.B.H.

PART ONE

1.

A NEW APPROACH TO AN OLD IDEA

'Oneself I sing, a simple, separate person.'
Walt Whitman

'The proper study of mankind is man.'
Pope

In that most popular form of literature, the detective story, the reader's attention is focused always on one central question — WHO committed the crime? The culprit is the point of interest, not what was done or how it was accomplished. The tangled complexities of the plot clear up like magic with the discovery of the individual who was the cause of it all.

It seems that when it comes to unravelling everyday problems we find that life is very much like a detective story, not only in its complexities, but also in the fact that events — great and small, international or domestic, catastrophic or trifling — are caused primarily by the actions of some individual person. History shows, again and again, that one man can overturn the world, and contemporary experience has borne out this truism rather grimly. Everybody knows that a single member of the family can destroy the happiness of a home, that one of the partners in a firm can wreck a sound business, and that just one inharmonious guest can wreck a party.

Equally it is true that no situation has ever been saved except through the action of an individual. Some one person is always at the centre, or out in front, of everything that happens, from a world war to a motor accident, from great industrial or national achievements to the happiness of children or the culture of better blueberries.

It is therefore a curious fact that in spite of the enormous progress of science in almost every field of practical living, very little is known about the basic psychological structure of the individual, or, more simply, why people behave and misbehave the way they do. The world is still surprised when some obscure person rises abruptly to power, or when a public idol topples from his pedestal. Most of all, in the intimate matters of everyday human relationships, our inability to understand each other lies at the bottom of the greater number of our perplexities. We also suffer from our inability to understand ourselves.

The old proverb says 'to understand all is to forgive all,' but a more practical version would be 'to understand all is to be able to handle the situation better.' It has always been believed that if some method or formula could be found by which we could *know* — without having to learn through misunderstandings, unhappiness, and even tragedy — the people we love, live with, work with, and encounter in the course of our daily lives, it might well be that life in general could develop into a more manageable affair. And if such a formula were available, it could be applied not only to other people, but to ourselves. One of the most persistent ideas of civilized mankind is the theory that if we could 'know ourselves' we would be better off.

In this book there is set forth a simple, workable formula for understanding and analyzing people — other people and ourselves. This formula is a blend of ancient and modern ideas; it is a new application of an old hypothesis. The new formula has been in practical use for nearly forty-five years, and its application, in relation to thousands of individuals, has added considerable strength to the age-old belief in the value of self-knowledge — as well as providing an efficient short-cut to the more modern objective of getting a line on the other fellow. It replaces the somewhat egotistic ideal of making friends and influencing people by the simpler objective of being yourself and understanding other people.

Considerable effort has been expended by modern psychologists, educationalists, and industrialists, on the problem of analyzing human personality. Many interesting results have been obtained, and popularized through books and articles: methods of type classifications, character tests, intelligence tests, mental ratings, and many others. The methods, as a rule, are designed for professional use, and as they vary considerably, both in the factors employed and in results, they are not of much use to the untrained layman, that is, to the average person. They do not help you and me to understand why one of us is happy digging in the garden and wretched if called upon to propose an after-dinner toast, while another doesn't know a rosebush from a cabbage, but yearns for public opportunity and power.

Nor do these widely differentiated methods of personality analysis give us any clue to that greater mystery — human relationships. They do not explain why one person is instantly congenial to you but antagonistic to me, why one marriage is successful while another fails, or why some families get along harmoniously together and others resemble a menagerie of badly assorted wild animals. More than this, no method of understanding people has been offered to the modern world that suggests in any way the existence of an orderly plan or pattern for the human scheme of things. The background of our immediate physical universe appears, in the light of modern science, to exhibit a satisfying order, from the solar system to the atom. But of the psychological structure of humanity we can only say with Shakespeare, '*a mad world, my masters!*' and let it go at that

These very problems, however, have been of deep concern to mankind at different periods in the past. Whenever a high degree of civilization produces wealth and leisure, scholarship and culture develop. During these peaks of culture, as history shows, there has been always a great awakening of interest in the mental and spiritual structure of the individual human being. But because of the curious persistence of the human race in destroying everything that is created by each upward wave of civilization, much of the knowledge gathered by the scholars of antiquity has been lost, and many people believe that no such knowledge ever existed — that the first scientific age of history began with Darwin.

Enough of ancient knowledge has survived, however, to suggest that the existence of a true scientific spirit, long prior to modern times, is a fact and not a myth. Historians tell us that during the last great peak of culture preceding the Dark Ages — the Alexandrian Period, just before Caesar and the Roman Empire — the sciences, especially mathematics and astronomy, had reached a high level of development along with the recognized achievements of the period in the arts, poetry and philosophy.

It was in certain remaining records of this ancient science that the nucleus of a new formula for analyzing individual personality was found. The basis of this formula belongs to the knowledge of antiquity, but its development and application have been considerably rationalized by the findings of modern physics. Without the light thrown upon the ancient hypothesis by recent developments in the field theory of relativity the formula would have remained an even deeper mystery than it is. For, although it gives results with almost mathematical accuracy, our formula still retains the element of mystery — which is not incompatible with the modern scientific viewpoint. Einstein himself stated that in physics, it is *not properties but probabilities* which are described.

In order to use a formula, of course, we do not have to understand it — as witnessed by the story of $e^{i\pi}+1=0$ quoted in the foreword. Nobody knows what electricity is, but by the discovery of one formula after another, since Ben Franklin flew his famous kite, electricity has become the servant of mankind. We probably use the fourth dimension every day of our lives, but nobody understands it. Edward Kasner, in *Mathematics and the Imagination*, rebukes us for what he calls 'our rather childish desire for consistency.'[1]

The ancient theory of birthdate-conditioning underlying the new formula is one which has survived since the dawn of history. Being a bit hoary, it naturally has gathered, during the course of uncounted centuries, a good deal of extraneous matter — like moss on an old tree. In spite of these appendages, however, the theory itself has survived with persistent vitality, and has experienced, in recent years, a noticeable rejuvenation through a sudden increase of public interest in its most familiar manifestation. The basis of the theory is that in addition to other recognized conditioning factors of character and personality — such as heredity, environment, and training — there exists in the human scheme of things a psychological conditioning factor that is related to the individual's birthdate.

Any suggestion as to the conditioning of human affairs, either in the mass or individually, by the mere fact of a period of time, has been considered by most modern thinkers as being beyond the pale of credibility. Banned by the Church in the early centuries of Christianity, 'astrology' at that period became a forbidden subject. In our own time, the mechanistic approach of science to human problems, dating from the days of Darwin, has precluded any acceptance of the postulate that man was a part of the natural scheme of things, and that by the mere virtue of being born, he held a certain, definite place of his own in that scheme, within which he had an inalienable right to the pursuit of his own happiness.

This agreeable and self-respecting idea was frowned on by early 20th-century science, just as it was banned — to the point of burning at the stake — by the early Church. (We moderns do not burn our astrologers, but we have been known to put them in jail.) The historical details of this angle of the subject are so full of interest that they deserve a chapter to themselves, which will be found in the later pages of this book. At the moment, however, it is sufficient to state that while the new formula is based on the ancient time-conditioning theory, the present approach to the idea is one which has not been presented before — to the best of the writer's knowledge — and that the formula shows enough correlation with certain findings of modern physics to suggest that somewhere, at the heart of the idea, there lies a germ of scientific truth.

The principal difference between the traditional ideas about birthdate-conditioning and the cycle formula is obvious. While the traditional theories place the causation factors vaguely 'in the heavens' and loosely describe them as 'the stars', the theory on which the new formula is based brings the whole matter down to earth, and links it with familiar terrestrial phenomena. The possibility of a truly scientific correlation between certain fundamentals of the ancient pattern of birthdate-conditioning and the more modern developments in physics is another part of the subject which requires a chapter to itself. The scientifically minded reader will find in Chapter 4, Part III some interesting suggestive evidence that 'modern' psychology may be the legitimate offspring of a much older science, and that the structure of the 'electrical universe' of present-day physics was familiar ground to the scholars of antiquity.

Briefly, and merely by way of introduction to the formula itself, the tentative principle behind the whole idea of birthdate-conditioning is something like this:

We live in the world, as human beings, because the earth is suited to our essential needs. It provides us with food to eat, clothes to cover us, and air to breathe. The latter — air — would seem to be the most essential. Unless we can breathe, our other faculties are cancelled out.

The atmosphere surrounding the earth, under a great many different names, has always been, and still is, a matter of special interest to scientific research. Some of the most recent discoveries of physics concerning it suggest that we are living within *a field of energy* which surrounds and envelops the earth like an invisible halo, shot through with electrical charges. So it seems that not only does this mysterious field supply us with air to breathe; it does much more. From its energy we charge the batteries of our nerves and sinews, so that we may function successfully in our normal sphere as earth-dwellers. Einstein stated that to the physicist, this field is as real as the chair on which he sits.

Science today has many methods of measuring the physical effects of these electrical charges. Certain facts, pertinent to the cycle formula, seem to have emerged from these measurements. One is that the energy of the earth's field is always in a state of change. Another, that the changes in the field appear to be related to changes in solar radiation — that is, that the sun is the most important factor in the creation of earthly atmospheric conditions. And another, still in the tentative stage, is that the cyclic changes in this field *may* have a measurable effect on psychological human reactions, and are possibly related to observable changes in mass psychology.

Millions of dollars are being spent annually in the study of solar radiation and its possible practical relationships to human life and problems. Dr H. T. Stetson, of the Massachusetts Institute of Technology, has said:

'The sun is certainly the most important star to us as human beings living on this planet earth ... We are able to live on this earth of ours only because the earth's distance from the sun is such that we get just the right amount and quality of radiation from the sun to make life possible ... *That changes in the sun may momentarily affect the balance of the various factors influencing human behavior may be speculative but not at all impossible.* On such a basis it will do us no harm to venture our imaginations. It may be surprising to find in how many different ways changes in the sun are reflected in affairs on earth.'[2]

The ancient systems of birthdate and time-conditioning, when analyzed and reduced down to their fundamentals, are found without exception to be based on the solar year — that is, on the regular relationship between the earth and the sun. While different civilizations of the past — Chinese, Hindu, Egyptian, Greek, Arabian, Medieval European, and others — have left scattered records of a great variety of patterns and divisions in their many time-conditioning systems, they are all agreed on one point: that the basis of the whole matter is the solar year. Most of us learned in school that the solar year, which we normally measure off in seasons, months, and weeks, according to the calendar, is created by one complete revolution of the earth around the sun. The revolutions of the other members of the sun's family — the planets — with which we are also familiar from schooldays, are incidental to the great central fact of the earth's annual revolution around the sun, which, science suggests, is the main causal factor in the creation of the all-important field of the earth. [3]

The four seasons constitute the fundamental, natural divisions of the year. Other divisions, varying in duration, have been added from time to time by the makers of calendars. Modern astronomy, however, still uses the traditional method of dividing the circle of the year into twelve sections, each period covering 30 of the 360 degrees that make up the circumference of the celestial sphere. The apparent 'yearly journey' of the sun through the celestial sphere, as observed from the earth, determines these degrees, even though we know that the sun's 'journey' is an optical illusion. And modern astronomy continues to use the symbolic names given to the twelve 30-degree periods of the year by the ancients, which are known familiarly to us as the twelve signs of the zodiac. [4]

The ten-day cycle formula of birthdate-conditioning likewise is based on the fundamental structure of the solar year. It springs from the general premise of the scientists of antiquity that changes in the aspect of the celestial sphere, induced by the constantly shifting positions of the sun's family of planets — including, of course, the earth — have a *psychological* as well as a *physical* effect on human conditions, and that, therefore, the point in time of one's birthdate could be held to influence one's psychological structure. Call the *celestial sphere* the *field*, and this idea becomes more reasonable.

What the ancients really called this sphere of influence we do not know, but modern science has a name for it. While no physicist, as yet, officially agrees with the hypothesis of time-conditioning, neither has any physicist been found who can officially disprove it. For it seems, upon reflection, that the celestial sphere of influence in which the ancient scientists believed so firmly, and which they linked with the idea of *time* in so many different ways, may be what modern science calls the *four-dimensional space-time continuum*. Dr C. G. Jung, in his famous statement on the psychological values of 'astrology', called the sphere of influence simply 'a continuum of time', and explains its influence by saying that '*what is born or done in any moment of time has the qualities of that moment of time*'.[5]

Unlike traditional 'astrology', the ten-day cycle formula gives no specific psychological value to the zodiacal signs themselves. The formula is based on a mathematical relationship between the *four* major divisions of the ancient universe — which were called 'elements' — and a series of *thirty-six* ten-degree cycles of the year, each cycle being approximately ten days in length.

It has been found, through the study and correlation of all the factors involved in this ten-day cycle formula — the history and sources of which are fully described in Chapter 4 — that during the period of each ten-day cycle there is a predominant psychological quality, a prevalent mood or feeling, which shows itself, in relation to mass psychology, in the way people respond to what is going on. With reference to individual psychology, it has been found that the people who are born during any one of the ten-day cycles — all of which are specifically timed — will reflect in their personalities the basic psychological qualities belonging to the cycle which includes their birthdates, irrespective of their year, or place of birth, or of the time of day they are reported to have emitted their first cry of protest against the event.

In accepting the phrase *belonging to the cycle* it seems that the reader is being asked to take a good deal for granted. But we must remember $e^{i\pi}+1=0$. And if the reader will peruse, later, the story of where, and how, the details of these psychological factors were discovered, correlated, tested, and proved as far as any personality formula can be proved — by the practical application of its factors to a number of individuals over a considerable period of time — their rather amazing accuracy will be more easily credible.

What the formula reveals about the individuals whose birthdays occur during the specified periods of the cycles is their fundamental, natural response to the basic challenges of life.

It has been said that life is made up of three main challenges — sex, work, and social relationships, which would seem to cover the practical problems of everyday living with clarity and efficiency. The ten-day cycle formula goes a step further; it expands and develops this triplicity of challenges. The formula provides three principal factors, or ingredients, in the structure of each personality portrait, which function in each individual according to what might be called a psychological ratio.

These three fundamental factors are called, in the formula, the BASIC QUALITY, the POTENTIAL, and the FREQUENCY.

The ancient scholars, as has been said, divided everything in life into *four* great divisions, to which they gave the symbolic names of Fire, Water, Air and Earth. These four symbols are used in the ten-day cycle formula to indicate *basic qualities* — the fundamental response of the individual to the three-fold challenges of love, earning a living, and getting along with other people. These four qualities underlie, in each case, the functioning of the other two formula factors, as well as the additional existing factors of physical conditioning and environment.

Every ten-day cycle falls definitely into one or another of these four groups. It is interesting to note in this connection that Pythagoras, in the 7th century BC, and Dr C. G. Jung, in our own time, came to similar conclusions that humanity can be divided into four basic psychological types, or groups[6] and that modern medicine recognizes four, and only four basic blood groups or types. The four basic types constitute the fundamental structure of the formula.

Next in importance, in the formula pattern, comes a conditioning factor designed by a number. As there are 36 cycles in the solar year, and 4 basic qualities, the mathematical expectancy would be that there are 9 cycles related, or belonging to each of the 4 qualities. This is exactly the way the pattern works itself out, with a most interesting extension of the matter of the numbers used in the formula. These are not merely numbers; they are attributed to the spot cards of the familiar pack with which we play poker and bridge — and tell fortunes. The cards used are those from the TWOS to the TENS. The Aces are discreetly left out, the inference being, possibly, that in the human family Aces are made, not born! The pack of cards referred to by the ancient scholars is, of course, the medieval pack, known as the TAROT, which was the precursor of the modern pack, and probably its original. The basis of the formula was discovered in a medieval document of unknown origin, containing detailed descriptions of every card in the Tarot pack.*

The origin and meaning of the pack of cards has always been a mystery of great interest to historians. The ten-day cycle formula serves to throw new light on the question of why the pack of cards is constructed as it is, who constructed it, and the possible object of its invention. This question, too, requires a chapter to itself, which will be found later in the book. In passing, let us merely recall the rather pertinent statement made by Alice — just as she was growing to her full size, and leaving Wonderland for reality — that the human race is *nothing but a pack of cards*. Lewis Carroll, who created Alice, was a mathematician in his leisure moments, and many people have suspected that behind the Carroll fantasies lurk hidden truths.

For the practical purposes of the formula — the understanding of people — these formula numbers from the pack of cards are very useful. To each number is attributed a definite psychological *potential*. This is a quality of psychological energy, or power, which turns out to be a vital factor in the structure of the personality. Each ten-day cycle has its own specific number, and is linked with a certain card in the ancient Tarot pack.

The third series of factors in the formula is symbolized by the names of the six nearest planets of the solar system, and the sun. It cannot be too strongly emphasized that *these are only symbols*, and have nothing whatever to do with the heavenly bodies. The order in which these symbols stand in the pattern is arbitrary, and is given in many of the oldest systems of alchemy and 'astrology'. It seems likely that these symbols indicate the timing of a series of changes, or waves of solar radiation, within the 'field' of the year, changes which induce a human response corresponding to the emotional impulse traditionally represented by the mythological deities for whom the planets are named. Because the factors in this third series evidently stand for emotions, they have been called, in the formula, *frequencies* — borrowing a term from physics which means, broadly, the speed of a vibration.

*See Chapter 3 Part III.

These three sets of factors make up the structure of the ten-day cycle formula.

In using the formula, it should be kept in mind that birthdate-conditioning is only one of a number of normal conditioning factors affecting the individual. It would seem, from its very nature, that birthdate-conditioning should provide the more basic, integral, and innate characteristics of the personality, and this has been found to be the case. These integral factors can show themselves in as many different ways, on the surface, as there are individual human beings in the world. No two individuals ever had *all* the conditioning factors of life alike — not even identical twins.

But it has been found — and will be found as readers study the correlated psychological portraits of their own birthday cycles along with those of people known intimately to them, of their acquaintances, and associates, and of famous people whose characteristics are common knowledge — that the ten-day cycle formula gives a fundamentally accurate picture of the true psychological personality of any individual born within the period of any given cycle.

More than this — the formula sets forth a picture, not of 'a mad world, my masters', but of a world where people are suddenly revealed as being part of an orderly, balanced scheme of things, completely free in their pursuit of destiny, but with confidence in 'the inner harmony of the world'.

If it can be recognized — or even imagined! — that every individual has his own place, his own path, his own orbit, in the human universe, in which his heart's desire *can* be achieved, his destiny and happiness pursued in the freedom of his own inalienable right to be himself, the rediscovery of the ten-day cycle pattern, and its development into a practical formula for the personal use of every one of us, will have fulfilled a constructive and a satisfying purpose.

Notes:
1. See *Mathematics and the Imagination* by Edward Kasner and James Newman. Simon & Schuster, 1940.
2. *Sun Spots and their Effects* by Harlan True Stetson (pages 10-11) McGraw-Hill, 1937.
3. See *Scientific Progress*, by Sir James Jeans and others (page 96). Macmillan, 1936.

4. The Twelve Signs of the Zodiac are: Aries, Taurus, Gemini, Cancer, Leo, Virgo, Libra, Scorpio, Sagittarius, Capricorn, Aquarius, Pisces.
5. See *The Secret of the Golden Flower* by Richard Wilhelm, with commentary by C. G. Jung (page 143), Harcourt, Brace, 1931.
6. *Psychological Types* by C. G. Jung (page 14). Harcourt, Brace, 1933; and *Collectanea Hermetica* (Vol. 9, page 15).

2.

THE ORDER OF THE FORMULA

'The world walls made a vast square, the type of all perfect gardens
and cloisters, the enclosure four-square, in which, according to the
Avesta, man was first placed . . . Would you know the new, you must
search the old.'

W. R. Lethaby

The structure of the ten-day cycle formula is very simple, in that it
deals only with the fundamental impulses, desires, and reactions
of the individual. It does not point to one season as a producer of
genius, another as a breeding-ground for the feebleminded. Genius
can spring from any point in the year's pattern, and so can mediocrity
and folly.

The formula indicates, by the *basic quality*, the *potential*, and the
frequency, the three principal psychological ingredients, or factors,
of every individual according to the cycle of his or her birthdate. What
any individual chooses to do with his own personal factors is entirely
up to himself. The function of the formula is to indicate what these
factoral ingredients are, in every individuality, and to suggest how
the best use can be made of them, both in the practical solving of
everyday problems and in the broad approach to life.

In formulating here the principal factors of the personality portraits
of the thirty-six cycles, the symbols of the ancient science have been
retained where possible, rather than translating them into modern
expression. There is beauty and charm in the older symbols; they
are familiar today to almost everybody. And it seems that we owe
it to the ancient scientists to retain something of the language in which
they bequeathed us their record. Also, the ten-day cycle pattern is
based on the astronomical, not the calendar year, so that the symbols

are accurate in time. The twelve signs of the zodiac, as well as the approximate calendar dates, are given in each case as the most appropriate background for allocating the cycles in their proper periods, and the mythological names, in the case of the frequencies, are used to add colour to the picture. Each ten-day cycle is titled with the combination of a number and a sign, which gives it a conveniently brief identification.

The Tarot cards are included to complete the picture of the original structure as found in the source document, BOOK T, which is described in some detail in Chapter 3 Part III. In this document each ten-day cycle is described in terms of one of the spot cards of the Tarot pack. The specific symbols of the card — the suit and number — correlate with the basic quality and the potential of each cycle. The mythological, or planetary symbols of the frequencies are given in the descriptions of the cards, but are not found on the cards themselves in the pack from which these designs were sketched. This is known as the Waite pack, and it was selected from the various packs available today because of its use of symbolic human figures. These figures seem to suggest, more directly than is done in other designs, the evident psychological quality of the spot-card descriptions. The attitudes, actions, and expressions of the symbolic figures, in most cases, fit the general personality of the cycle rather closely, and thus the cards are of value, as well as of interest, in the interpretation of the symbols and descriptions.

The four basic qualities

These constitute the broad foundation of the personality structure, and their importance in understanding the instinctive approach to life, either in other people or in oneself, can hardly be overestimated. Any cycle, irrespective of modification by its potential and frequency, will be found to induce the characteristic response of its basic quality in the personality of every individual born during the period.

The four basic types of the formula are found to conform both with the ancient Pythagorean pattern and with the modern Jungian pattern of personality. Ancient science allocated all the phenomena of life and nature to the four 'elements', including personality types, and it is interesting to discover that Dr Jung's divisions, which are based on a lifetime of psychological practice and research, correspond perfectly with the Pythagorean plan and with the four basic qualities of the formula. The formula qualities are here translated from the symbols as clearly as can be done in a single word or phrase, and the multiple correlation may be tabulated thus:

Ancient Symbol	Pythagoras	Jung	The Formula (Basic Quality)
FIRE	IMAGINATION TYPE	FEELING TYPE	DYNAMIC ENERGY
WATER	INTUITION TYPE	THINKING TYPE	FLEXIBILITY
AIR	REASON TYPE	INTUITION TYPE	MENTALITY
EARTH	SENSATION TYPE	SENSATION TYPE	PRACTICAL SENSE

What this implies is that all individuals born during any one of the ten-day cycles attributed to a certain basic type in the formula will exhibit in their personalities the basic qualities of that type.

The words here chosen to describe the four basic qualities are scarcely adequate, but they represent the closest approximation in words to the significance of these qualities, as factors of individuality, that could be found after years of search for the perfect phrase. There is a new and modern science called 'semantics', which studies the proper use of words, and nowadays is popular. But in the task of translating the ten-day cycle formula into words the writer has come to respect more and more the habit of the ancients in using symbols rather than phrases to express profound ideas. When the science of semantics is as dead as alchemy and the dodo, we will still speak of a man as 'fiery' or 'earthy' and our meaning will be understood. 'Airy' and 'watery' are not quite so obvious as type-symbols until they have become familiar through use. But the connotation of mental agility with *air*, and of receptive, yielding flexibility with *water*, do not demand too great a stretch of the imagination.

The twelve signs of the zodiac are evenly divided among the four 'elements'. There are *three* signs, each containing three ten-day cycles, allocated to each element. These are distributed at regular intervals along the pattern of the year, which begins, traditionally, with March 21st. Each sign covers a time period of approximately thirty days, actually 30 degrees.

FIRE	EARTH	AIR	WATER
PERIODS	PERIODS	PERIODS	PERIODS
Aries	Taurus	Gemini	Cancer
Leo	Virgo	Libra	Scorpio
Sagittarius	Capricorn	Aquarius	Pisces

FIRE: People born during any one of the nine ten-day cycles of Aries, Leo, or Sagittarius will exhibit the basic quality of dynamic energy — a positive, direct approach to life, tending more toward impulsive action and emotional response than is the case with the other three qualities.

WATER: The Water cycles of Cancer, Scorpio, and Pisces tend to induce a somewhat slower reaction — a quieter, more patient approach than with the other qualities. Individuals with birthdays in the Water cycles are usually more inclined to receptivity than to positive action; they are mentally and emotionally more flexible, impressionable, and intuitive than are the other three types.

AIR: People born during the cycles of Gemini, Libra, or Aquarius exhibit a greater clarity of mind than those in the other basic groups. That is, to use the old phrase, 'their heads rule their hearts' instead of the other way round. This does not mean that they are clever while everybody else is stupid — far from it. Thinking is just as apt to be the wrong thing to do as feeling, acting, or following a hunch; it all depends on how it is done. The 'air' people instinctively try to think before they act; it is their natural approach to life.

EARTH: Without these cycles in the pattern the world would be in a bad way. People born during the nine cycles of Taurus, Virgo, and Capricorn are the natural possessors of what we call common sense — whether they use it or not. They are the integrators, the practical, constructive workers, and it is when they branch off in unnatural directions that they find themselves in trouble. 'Earth' people can be poets and mystics just as well as the rest of us, but they always feel a need to integrate their dreams in practical and constructive form in order to be true to themselves.

Always, in every case, the basic quality is modified by the other two main factors of the ten-day cycle — the potential and the frequency. It is in the specific statement of the result of the combination of these factors, of their blending into a composite which creates a unified, balanced personality, that the charm and ingenuity of the ten-day cycle formula begin to appear.

The nine numbers — the potentials

The potentials indicate the driving force of the personality. They modify, and are modified by the accompanying factors, but they are unmistakable in their effect on the quality of drive and energy in the individual's way of life. The detailed interpretation of the cycles themselves makes the significance of the potentials clearer than any explanation can do, but an attempt at tabulation gives the following correlation of numbers and characteristics:

TWO   — Initiative, adaptability, uncertainty.
THREE — Determination, intensity, pride.
FOUR   — Stability, order, restriction.
FIVE   — Activity, power, opposition.
SIX   — Ambition, leadership, egocentricity.
SEVEN — Versatility, dominance, fear.
EIGHT — Sagacity, prudence, shortsightedness.
NINE   — Forcefulness, capability, obstinacy.
TEN   — Persistence, conservatism, self-will.

The seven frequencies

The frequencies represent the type of desire, or quality of emotion characteristic of people born during each cycle. The symbols used are mythological, and refer to the supposed characteristics of the gods and goddesses having the names of the seven planets of the solar system. As noted elsewhere, the frequencies have nothing to do with the planets; the formula pattern is based entirely on the cyclic changes in the field of the earth, through its relationship with the sun, during the course of the solar year. The gods, in ancient times, symbolized human emotions and desires, which are tricky things to trap in words. But by virtue of the basic, traditional meanings of the mythological symbols, their correlations work out something like this:

MARS   — desire for action; energy, impulsiveness.
SUN   — desire to achieve; ambition, pride.
VENUS   — desire to create; productivity, extravagance.
MERCURY   — desire to reason; sagacity, cunning.
MOON   — desire for change; adaptability, instability.
SATURN   — desire to integrate; constructiveness, intensity.
JUPITER   — desire to stabilize; order, caution.

The conflict

Growing out of the multiple correlations of the cycle formula is found, in every case, a clue to the fundamental conflict which, psychology tells us, is going on in the nature of every individual most of the time. Even when we are asleep, it seems, the conflict continues in our dreams — the opposing parts of our nature at war with one another, creating disharmony, unhappiness, inefficiency, and sometimes even illness.

The factors of the cycle formula suggest, through the different combinations of quality, potential, and frequency, the basis of this conflict in each case, and how it can be resolved without the necessity for calling upon anything more than our own natural psychological equipment.

Positive and negative

One of the most unique — and cheering — aspects of the ten-day cycle formula is that it presents both sides of our psychological natures with the utmost frankness and fairness, and entirely without prejudice. This open-minded approach to the tender subject of our faults and virtues reveals an interesting and encouraging idea behind the formula, which has proved to be both constructive and fundamentally true.

The psychologists of antiquity, who worked out the basis of the formula, evidently considered that our faults are nothing more than the obverse side of our virtues. We have the choice of going about the world right side out, or wrong side out, and except in the matter of practical results, we might never notice the difference. Most of us keep on making blunders, in spite of what we sincerely believe to be our best intentions. What we are really doing, under these conditions, is *functioning wrong side out*.

Instead of trying to change our natural approach — to behave, that is, like someone else — the formula shows that the best way to correct the error of our ways is by examining our own individual actions and reactions under the new light of our two-way personality portrait, and then by adhering to the positive side of the picture at all times. This is the object of the double analysis, *positive* and *negative*, given in the description of each one of the cycles. The achievement of equilibrium between our positive and negative characteristics, our right and wrong sides, can be achieved, as a rule, by the deliberate, conscious development of our positive characteristics — by keeping right side out. But the formula, as will be seen, goes one step further, and supplies some interesting and helpful suggestions which are given, in each case, under the head of *balance*.

A word or two of warning must be added.

This series of thirty-six personality portraits does *not* limit the scope of human possibilities within the bounds of thirty-six separate and distinct receptacles, like modern medicine bottles with their various ingredients listed precisely on the labels. At first glance, it might appear that the formula carries with it some such quality of limitation, but this is most emphatically not the case.

While there are, actually, only a few basic desires, emotions, and capacities of which the human race is capable — biologists tell us we are driven by only two urges, hunger and love — the structure of the ten-day cycle formula suggests, by the great diversity of inter-relationships between the basic human factors set forth in its four-by-nine pattern, the possibility of almost infinite variety in the expression and development of the individuals who make up the human family.

The subtle difference between the desire for power that produces a dictator and the desire to lead and guide that produces a great king or leader of men — the hairline that divides dishonesty from the desire to show off — the differentiation between cowardice and caution — these things, which create so much misunderstanding between human beings *because they are so hard to recognize* — are analyzed for us by the formula. They are indicated with extraordinary clarity — as will be seen — but with no sense of limiting an individual's possibilities by labelling him a dictator, a great leader, a hero, or a coward. As the kabalist Eliphas Levi — who undoubtedly was familiar with the basis of this formula — puts it: '*Every individuality is indefinitely perfectible*'.

The true value of the ten-day cycle formula would seem to lie in the fact that it shows us the component parts of our real natures, thus enabling us to be ourselves with conscious and intelligent purpose.

According to numerous authorities, from Elijah to Aldous Huxley, it is only by being ourselves that we may hope to attain the one goal eternally desired by civilized man. This goal is the freedom of the individual to pursue his own destiny in his own way.

Now and again, along the path of history, the goal is temporarily obscured by a blackout — such as totalitarianism — and the individualistic ideal seems lost. But always it returns, with renewed energy, to carry on the job of human progress. Ancient and modern history alike have shown this fact to be self-evident, and the American Declaration of Independence is one of its major consequences.

We are also told, however, that the price of freedom is eternal vigilance. Perhaps the Ten-Day Cycle Formula of birthdate-conditioning may be taken as a rediscovered document of individualism, showing the most constructive and effective path along which every human individual can exercise that eternal vigilance whose fruit is freedom.

PART TWO

THE TWELVE SIGNS OF THE ZODIAC AND THE THIRTY-SIX CYCLES

NOTE: In the case of birthdates that fall on the *last* day or the *first* day of a cycle as the dates are given here, there is sometimes a doubt as to which of the two cycles actually includes the birthday. This is because of the vagaries of the calendar. It is usually possible to come to an accurate decision by studying the personal factors of the two cycles. It will be found in all cases that every individual belongs definitely to one cycle or the other — there are no bordering, or composite personalities, in the ten-day cycle formula of birthdate-conditioning.

However, each group of *three* ten-day cycles falls within the boundaries of a thirty-day period involving one of the twelve familiar zodiac signs. Each person's zodiacal sign exerts a subtle inner quality which blends with the factors of personality in each ten-day cycle. This quality is illustrated by a Tarot KEY (preceding the cycles) traditionally symbolizing the zodiac sign of the group.

The names of well-known people listed in each of the birthdate cycles have been selected more or less at random as they came to the attention of the author. No statistical records of names and cycles have been attempted; these names serve only to illustrate the wide variety of individual expression possible to each birthdate cycle. Since all birthdates here mentioned have been taken from public records they are not guaranteed by the author.

THE EMPEROR.

ARIES
(March 21 to April 20)

His royal birthday gift, as spring breaks through the ice of winter, is a sense of personal power and individual responsibility. The will to take action — rather than wait — is balanced by a natural ability to *see*, clearly and logically, all sides of any problem or question that may arise. The Aries mind probes through surface impressions, so often erroneous, to the reality behind any situation, personal or collective. The Aries nature is so dynamic, so forceful, that this ability to discriminate between what is true and what may be false is a gift whose cultivation is essential — and is certain to be very fruitful.

TWO of ARIES

March 21 to 30   (0° to 9°59′ of ♈)

Potential: TWO   Frequency: MARS
(Initiative)   *(Activity)*
Basic Quality: FIRE
(Dynamic Energy)

Activity, resourcefulness, enthusiasm, and adaptability are the basic factors in this personality. The conflict lies between the urge to action and a desire for inner equilibrium, or peace.

On the positive side
There is a stimulating, vitalizing quality in the nature of the Aries TWOS. They are always ready for action and adventure. They are eager to take the lead, willing to accept responsibility. They are courageous, positive and direct in their approach to life. Their emotions are powerful; they are deeply affectionate and passionately loyal. They are attractive to, and attracted by, the opposite sex. They have an instinctive human tolerance; they adapt themselves with ease to any social or intellectual level. They are very generous, sharing not only their possessions but their vitality with others.

On the negative side
They are over-positive and dominating. Their initiative turns wrong side out to impetuosity, their courage to recklessness and a disregard of consequences. They start many more things than they can finish, and leave a trail of uncompleted gestures. They are indecisive; unable to make up their minds between two courses of action. Tolerance reverts to lack of discrimination in the choice of friends and of channels of activity; their strong personal emotions get out of control and run riot. They develop a self-willed obstinacy which functions entirely without reason. When negative, they are easily hurt, over-sensitive to impressions, and very unforgiving.

Balance
High ideals, self-control, patience, and unfailing discrimination, are the best balancing factors for this highly-strung personality. Self-discipline is always demanded by the Mars frequency, and here the need for it is doubled by the dynamic force of the Fire quality in the personality. Equilibrium of mind and body, which is so greatly desired by every Aries TWO, can best be achieved from the inside out — beginning with simple self-control in the small things of everyday life, and working up to a rigorous control of the emotions, especially of jealousy and anger.

Comment
The people born during this first spring cycle are found to have great

difficulty in maintaining a sufficiently even keel to hold their course
— even after they have overcome the initial difficulty of every TWO,
which is to make up the mind what course to follow. They are not
naturally logical; they see both sides of a question with equal clarity,
and one of the hardest jobs on earth for an Aries TWO is to reach
a logical decision between two alternatives.

It has been found that their best decisions are made through
intuition, rather than by 'thinking things through'. They have a keen,
instinctive understanding of people and conditions that is a far more
reliable guide than their restless, volatile minds. When self-control
and discrimination are developed, and the personality well balanced,
the intuitive faculty grows so strong that it is almost like a sixth sense,
just as available for use as any of the other five. And it has been found
that the opposite is true: when an Aries TWO loses control of the
emotions, or relaxes the standards of ethics and behaviour, this
intuitive gift disappears and is lost.

The most successful outlet for the energies of the Aries TWOS
seems to lie in socialized activities. They work best, and are healthiest
and happiest, when they are with other people, and have plenty of
scope for physical energy. Working alone, or in sedentary
occupations, they become highly nervous, and their negative
tendencies of impatience, anger, and instability tend to dominate.

The record of birthdates in this cycle shows a high average of
famous people, covering many fields of achievement. Outstanding
examples are J. S. Bach, sublime composer; Marcel Marceau, brilliant
French mime artist; Arturo Toscanini, the great orchestra conductor;
A. E. Housman, English poet; Paul Verlaine, French poet; Robert
Frost, American poet; three painters: Van Dyck, Flemish; Vincent
Van Gogh, Dutch; and Francisco Goya, Spanish. The great scientist,
Steinmetz; the astrologer, Dane Rudhyar; and 'timeless' stars Joan
Crawford, Gloria Swanson, and Diana Ross grace this cycle.

They are notable for their courage and enthusiasm, for their quick
reactions. The resourcefulness makes them good in emergencies;
under stress, their intuition functions quickly, and there is no lag
between decision and action. Out of control, of course, this very
faculty makes them impetuous, impulsive, and careless of
consequences, but under control, the innate combination of courage
and initiative makes the Aries TWO a fine and splendid character,
with qualities of true heroism.

In personal relationships, they are successful as long as they guard against the tendency to sit always in the driver's seat. This tendency to take the initiative at all times has been found to break up homes and partnerships, ruin friendships, and create rifts between parents and children. When balanced, however, the Aries TWOS are charming companions, good parents, and devoted friends. They have an inherent capacity for practical achievement — the Tarot promises them 'strength, dominion, harmony of rule, and justice', and names their card '*Dominion*', implying control over life.

'Dominion'

THREE of ARIES

March 31 to April 10   (10° to 19°59′ of ♈)

Potential: THREE   Frequency: SUN
(Determination)   *(Ambition)*

Basic Quality: FIRE
(Dynamic Energy)

Idealism, a keen sense of beauty, intensity, and a desire for

achievement, are the outstanding factors in this personality.
The conflict lies between idealism and ambition.

On the positive side
There is a driving power of great intensity in this personality, mitigated
by a natural poise and dignity. The Aries THREES have strong
magnetic charm, a personal attraction that can draw to them the
things — and people — that they really want. They are ambitious,
constructive workers, energetic, enthusiastic, and eager. They have
a strong sense of integration; they finish everything they undertake,
and they are instinctive individualists. They have the gift of creating
a happy atmosphere round them wherever they are; they radiate
warmth and vitality, like the Sun. They are anxious always to alleviate
suffering or sorrow in their environment, and are impatient with evil
or ugliness. They are fundamentally idealists, looking always for the
best, and willing to work hard to attain their objectives.

On the negative side
Dignity and ambition turn wrong side out to pride and arrogance;
their personal magnetism attracts enemies instead of friends, failure
instead of success. When such a powerful attractive force turns
negative, it repels, pushing away people, opportunity and happiness.
A streak of cruelty appears; a disregard of other people's feelings.
Their individualism becomes a self-centred self-will; they are single-
minded, deaf to reason or argument. Their force of attraction hardens,
creating an obstacle both for the person concerned and for other
people. When negative, they create unhappiness. They exert a
powerful influence over their environment, because of their dynamic
force and great intensity.

Balance
Harmonious activity, friendliness, and consideration for others help
to tip the balance to the positive side of the scale, which is vitally
necessary for this highly-charged personality. Dignity, self-respect,
and idealism should be encouraged — but not allowed to run riot.
Tolerance is another excellent balancing quality for these
individualistic personalities, along with the cultivation of a
willingness to make the best of things as they are — even while

missing no opportunity to make them better. The practice of deliberate relaxation, to release the tensions, is the best of all balancing habits for the THREE of Aries.

Comment

By nature, these are important people, who take the centre of the stage as if by right. As a rule, no one objects to this, because they are usually very charming, scintillating, vividly agreeable personalities. They have self-confidence and dignity; the document calls it 'nobility'.

But the Aries THREES are individualists; their chief difficulty in life is to co-operate with other people. While they have a fine sense of showmanship, they usually put on their best shows when they can play the star parts. It has been found that they do not really want to lead, to direct, or to drive — they want to *shine*, like the Sun which symbolizes their frequency. This, of course, is often a difficult characteristic for other people to understand, and rouses antagonism and jealousy. But when it is understood, and skillfully used, this radiant quality becomes a definite asset, not only attracting good fortune to the individual, but also spreading an atmosphere of success and happiness which can be widely shared. The Aries THREES are basically generous; they are just as eager to share what they have with others as they are ambitious to play a notable part on life's stage.

There is a strong quality of persistence in the structure of this nature and a positive intensity. Otto Von Bismarck, Sergei Rachmaninoff, René Descartes, Franz Joseph Haydn, and Washington Irving are among the famous people born during this cycle. Algernon Swinburne, the nineteenth-century English poet, known for his romantic and sensual works; Baudelaire, French poet also infamous in his day for his romantic 'excesses' and sense of showmanship; and English poet William Wordsworth were all born during this period. The list also includes such supershowmen as Lowell Thomas, Harry Houdini, and Marlon Brando. Showmanship, carried far beyond the footlights, is illustrated by Casanova; and in another area, by Baba Ram Dass, former drug experimenter turned guru. Greatness of imagination and construction is illustrated by Hans Christian Andersen. In any walk of life, these are apt to be persons who stand out from the crowd.

When negative, they can be dangerous. They have a tendency to stifle and thwart ambition in other people, and their intolerance can be a menace not only to their own happiness and success, but that of the home or the general environment. It has been found, however, that because of their innate sympathy for suffering, and their keen desire to be successful in their own lives, that the positive side of this personality has a way of being predominant in most of the Aries THREES. Their friendly charm exerts a powerful balance on the right side of the scale.

The formula promises them 'success, completion of labour, realization of hope'. They have been found to succeed best in enterprises that call for constructive, creative work, and for the use of the imagination; they are happiest and most efficient when consolidating ideas into concrete form. They are never satisfied with ideas alone, or with dreams. They want to integrate their desires.

The Tarot document makes one very cheering suggestion about the Aries THREES. It credits them with 'the power of acquiring wealth'. This is encouraging, not only to the people born during this

'Established Strength'

cycle, but to the rest of us. For who knows but that in this picture and its symbols may be lurking a practical suggestion as to the best way of acquiring wealth, no matter when you happen to be born?

FOUR of ARIES

April 11 to 20   (20° to 29°59′ of ♈)

Potential: FOUR	Frequency: VENUS
(Stability)	*(Productivity)*

Basic Quality: FIRE
(Dynamic Energy)

Instinctive personal charm, a strong sense of justice, a desire for order and harmony, and a deep desire for happiness, make up the basic structure of this personality. The conflict is waged between the impulse for disciplined activity and production, and the laziness that is inherent in every VENUS frequency.

On the positive side
A logical mind, an active imagination, and a leaning toward the orthodox and conventional ways of life, combine to build here a personality that is well-balanced and at the same time very vital and attractive. The elemental emotions of the Venus frequency are stimulated by the FIRE quality, but well controlled by the orderly stability of the FOUR potential. There is, in this personality, a greater repose than in either of the other Aries cycles. The Aries FOURS have good judgment, discrimination, and self-reliance, along with a desire for fair dealing in human relationships and practical affairs. They are careful of details, honest, capable, and very orderly. They are versatile, and always instinctively generous and forgiving.

On the negative side
The logical mind becomes over-critical and bigoted, refusing to look beyond the narrow limits of its immediate environment. The desire for order turns to a sense of uneasiness, breaking down the charm and poise of the personality, inducing a nervous instability of purpose and a sulky discontent with everything in life. There is a lack of courage in the negative expression of the Venus frequency. Fear, in this basically dynamic and orderly picture, is out of place, and

consequently creates great disorder, turning discrimination and judgment into recklessness and folly. Versatility, ·vrong side out, results in a scattering of energies and lack of concentration.

Balance

The capability and charm of this personality can best be developed and encouraged by avoiding a sense of superiority to others, by tempering justice with mercy, and by cultivating a wide range of interests and knowledge. Control of the personal emotions is needed wherever the Venus frequency is found, but in this case there is a danger of inner conflict — because of the FOUR potential — from too much repression. These individuals need to give, and to seek, love and friendship, freedom from self-restriction, and to hold a broad, kindly viewpoint toward other people's ideas and reactions.

Comment

The greatest gift of this cycle to those who are born during its course is charm — that subtle thing currently called by a new name every season, and scientifically known as sex appeal. Colour of hair or eyes, or even a crippled body, makes no difference to its magic. This charm is found wherever the Venus frequency is a part of the birthdate pattern. It gives to the personality that irresistible attraction for the opposite sex which has nothing to do with any other factor than itself. In this cycle, the perilous nature of this gift is well balanced by the natural decorum of the FOUR potential, but it remains, nevertheless, the greatest asset, and the greatest danger, for the individuals born in mid-April.

In spite of their versatility, the orthodox occupations seem to be the most successful for the Aries FOUR — such as the law, banking, buying and selling, and domestic activities. Their love of order is tempered by their love of beauty. Thus, those born in mid-April are not personally ambitious; they want to get things done well, beautifully, and on time. The cycle's roll of fame is not a long one and includes perfectionists rather than flashing stars. One such literary perfectionist is Henry James, another is British historian Arnold J. Toynbee. The perfection of the founding documents of this nation reflect Thomas Jefferson's ideals, Jefferson also being an Aries FOUR. In show business there are such untiring performers as

Charlie Chaplin, Sir John Gielgud, and Peter Ustinov, all of whom fit the pattern in their 'trouble and labour' toward perfection of production and performance. The Aries FOURS really want happiness and security more than they desire the limelight of public success.

Lack of self-confidence is a factor frequently found among them, and personal studies have uncovered many an 'inferiority complex' lurking behind their outer poise and charm. This arises, probably, from their extraordinarily keen sense of order and justice. They are so anxious to be fair to other people that they forget to be fair to themselves. But, once started in any congenial enterprise, with self-confidence established, they are wonderfully creative and constructive workers. The Tarot document promises them 'perfection and completion, built up with trouble and labour'. The name of the card is 'Perfected Work'.

Women born in this cycle are excellent homemakers and hostesses; both men and women have a strong family and community loyalty. They have an innate ability for undertakings that have to do with

'Perfected Work'

feminine beauty, vanity, or conventional decoration. They are not adventurous by nature, and they are usually happier, healthier, and more successful when they follow the more beaten paths. But whatever they begin, they finish: anything undertaken by an Aries FOUR will be brought as close to the completion of perfection as is humanly possible.

TAURUS
(April 21 to May 20)

In accordance with his priestly disguise, the Hierophant bestows a birthday gift of spiritual, or inner *hearing* — a special sense that goes beyond the logical thinking of the Emperor. But, along with the indication of natural intuitive perception, the form of the picture calls for discipline and discrimination in following the dictates of your 'inner voice'. The Hierophant, even while giving you his blessing, and asking you to listen closely, warns you that throughout the world of nature — of which you are a part — and also within yourself, there are laws of order and harmony that must be complied with in order to achieve success and happiness.

FIVE of TAURUS

April 21 to 30   (0° to 9°59′ of ☿)

Potential: FIVE	Frequency: MERCURY
(Activity)	*(Sagacity)*

Basic Quality: EARTH
(Practical Sense)

Energy, courage, the spirit of reform, and active industry are the chief ingredients of this cycle. There is a sharp conflict here — an impetuous desire for action warring against a cautious, instinctive cunning and common sense.

On the positive side
There is a very powerful combination of factors in this cycle. The mixture of vigour and wit, of strength and cunning, with the practical sense of the Earth quality, induces a personality that seems, at times, to be capable of miracles. The Taurus FIVES have an instinctive understanding of human needs and wants; they have a strong desire to change and improve conditions. They have tremendous working energy and staying power; they are people of action, self-starters and self-chargers. They are good fighters, self-confident and fearless, and they have the ability to influence and inspire other people to positive action. They have a natural gift of speech, either in talking or writing; they know the power of words and how to use them.

On the negative side
The spirit of reform becomes the spirit of rebellion; in place of the desire to improve, to recreate, there is an urge to destroy, to tear down, regardless of damage or consequences. The passion for improvement reverts to a primitive anger against existing conditions, either in personal or general affairs. When negative, the Taurus FIVES take the opposition on principle, disagreeing with everyone; they throw obstacles in other people's way while breaking down, as they believe, the obstacles to their own progress. They are cruel, unreasonable, unyielding, and merciless, desiring personal power more than anything else in the world.

Balance
The three things most necessary to keep this personality on the safe side of the line are self-discipline, idealism, and strict honesty. When these three factors are applied to the reforming urge, its destructive qualities can be inhibited. By holding a high standard of ethics and behaviour, the dangers of the power complex can be avoided. And, when kept within the bounds of integrity, the brilliant mind of the Taurus FIVE can do great good, and can succeed in the very enterprise that is really the heart's desire of every one of them — to

make the world a better place to live in.

Comment
Considerable study of this cycle was necessary before the symbols, the discouraging picture on the card, and its name, could be satisfactorily interpreted. Why should 'Material Trouble' be applied to a personality of such evident force and power? Under analysis, the answer appears: one of the strongest factors in the nature of the Taurus FIVE is the desire to alleviate human suffering or privation — to 'change the sorry scheme of things entire'. This interpretation gives a basis for understanding the apparent contradiction in the symbols which has worked out with surprising logic in personal application.

It is difficult, today, to keep a cool viewpoint toward a birthdate cycle whose famous names include both Hitler and Lenin. Hitler was born in the evening of April 20, 1889, and the cycle, that year, changed during the day, making him unquestionably a Taurus FIVE. So it becomes necessary to add other names as fast as possible, such as Marconi, and three presidents of the United States: Grant, Buchanan, and Monroe. William Randolph Hearst is an interesting example of the power of the cycle. Other outstanding examples of the scope of this cycle are Queen of France Catherine de Medici; Queen Elizabeth II of England; English statesman Oliver Cromwell; and Russian revolutionist and founder of Soviet Union, Lenin. In literature we find Vladimir Nabokov, and Charlotte Brontë. In the performing arts we have Duke Ellington, Ella Fitzgerald, Barbra Streisand, Carol Burnett, and Shirley Temple. And last, we have the immortal bard, William Shakespeare, who has reigned for over three and a half centuries as the most important and brilliant FIVE of Taurus in the list, which is not, however, a particularly long one.

In everyday life, the happiest and most successful people born during this period have been found to be those whose activities are directed toward practical human needs — merchandising, supplying, or handling the regular commodities of life: managing homes and families. A socialized existence is usually best for the development of a Taurus FIVE; working or living alone, they tend to brood, and to become mystical and superstitious.

They are happiest when married, but the record of divorces in the cycle runs rather high, as also that of inveterate bachelors and bachelorettes. They have great charm, but a Mercury frequency always tends to chill the personal emotions, and in this case their somewhat combustible personal structure makes the Taurus FIVES, at times, rather hard to live with.

It seems to be unquestionable, however, that this cycle can produce a wonder-working genius, either for good or evil — as the magicians of ancient times were dedicated either to 'white, or to 'black' magic, according to whether their purposes were constructive or destructive. Marconi and Hitler, surely, are perfect examples of good and evil magicians. All of which suggests that to have a birthdate in this cycle implies quite a heavy responsibility!

'Material Trouble'

SIX of TAURUS

May 1 to 10   (10° to 19°59′ of ♉)

Potential: SIX   Frequency: MOON
(Ambition)   *(Adaptability)*
Basic Quality: EARTH
(Practical Sense)

Self-confidence, charm, independence, and imagination are the four pillars of this personal structure. The conflict is waged between the desire for fame and success, and a tendency to drift with the tide. This cycle stands at the peak of the first wave, inducing a powerful personality.

On the positive side

A great power of personal attraction, a fine sense of showmanship, and driving energy, are valuable assets to the Taurus SIXES. They are very independent; they have unlimited faith in themselves; they are determined to finish and complete anything they start. They are warmhearted, friendly, and liberal, always ready to share with others. They are idealists, demanding perfection in all things. They have an intuitive understanding of what the public wants (not, as with the FIVE, of its needs) and of ways to satisfy this desire. They have the ability to direct group activities, and their energy is vibrant and inspiring. Their imaginations are vivid and active, so much so that they possess an almost magical ability to give concrete form to their desires, to get what they want.

On the negative side

Pride becomes indolence, and showmanship turns to exhibitionism. Wrong side out, this individuality shows childish traits of vanity and boastfulness. Their adaptability becomes moody instability; they swing from the extreme of enthusiasm to that of pessimism, from hope to utter despair. They are unmanageable, self-willed, and headstrong. They use their intuitive knowledge of how people feel to hurt and wound the sensibilities of others. From being good directors, they become slave-drivers, developing a streak of almost sadistic cruelty. Generosity becomes extravagance, greed, and covetousness, which can even degenerate into an unethical attitude toward the responsibilities of life.

Balance

It is not easy for this forceful personality to achieve a balanced viewpoint. The method indicated is to develop the kindlier, gentler qualities; to follow a high standard of ethics and behaviour; to use the imagination for creating mental pictures that are constructive, beautiful, and hopeful. Discrimination in desire is the real secret of equilibrium and success for the Taurus SIX. They need to want the right things. They need, too, a life of activity, and the cultivation of a practical sense of responsibility in all departments of living.

Comment

This cycle holds a scientific interest, in that it is built up of an exact polarization of positive and negative forces. Six is the number, in the symbolic pattern, of the Sun, which is the most positive, masculine, or attractive of all the frequencies or potentials, while the Moon is the most negative, feminine, or expansive. This produces here a personality of polar opposites, and experience has produced much evidence that in people born during this period there is a strong tendency to go to extremes. They are either on the heights of ecstasy or in the depths of gloom — there is no middle way for the Taurus SIX.

In spite of its encouraging name, 'Material Success', the picture on the card warns the individual to balance charity with justice. This would seem to indicate that the personality is highly gifted, and that these gifts — abilities and potentialities — should not be squandered or wasted. The Tarot document describes the positive side of this nature as 'fortunate, successful, liberal, and just', and it promises, to all good Taurus SIXES, 'success in business, power, rule over the people'.

Showmanship is their greatest gift, and linked with the charm, the idealism, and the directive abilities natural to the personality, showmanship becomes a very practical weapon for success. Orson Welles, Judy Collins, Pete Seeger, Audrey Hepburn, and Fred Astaire are excellent examples of this special characteristic. They give evidence of the cycle's understanding of what the public wants and how to give it to them. One dictator, Robespierre, who plunged postrevolutionary France into a bloodbath and reign of terror, is on this list. To balance out this terrible extreme in the realm of government, we have the respected American president, Harry S. Truman. Also during this cycle we find the birthdays of five men who had a part in changing the world's thinking: Thomas Huxley, Soren Kierkegaard, Karl Marx, Sigmund Freud, and Niccolo Machiavelli.

In everyday life, the Taurus SIXES are either irresistibly charming or completely unmanageable, and sometimes both at once. They are usually popular, especially with the opposite sex. They are gregarious, hospitable, and social-minded. Except for a tendency toward fickleness in the closer personal affections, they are wonderful friends, and they can occupy with grace and ability the position of head of a family. They have a strong home-loving instinct, and home life is the best of all possible backgrounds for a Taurus SIX.

'Material Success'

SEVEN of TAURUS

May 11 to 20   (20° to 29°59′ of ♉)

Potential: SEVEN   Frequency: SATURN
(Versatility)   *(Intensity)*

Basic Quality: EARTH
(Practical Sense)

Imagination, determination, persuasiveness, and charm are the principal factors in this personality. The conflict is a very basic one: it is a fight between illusion and reality.

On the positive side
Broad vision, varied capacities, and natural personal charm are found in the right-side-out expression of this personality. The practical ability of the Taurus SEVENS is enhanced by a vivid, active imagination. Their personal charm, being instinctive, is particularly effective with the opposite sex, but it enables them at all times to make friends, and to influence other people. There is great power in their natures; they affect their environment strongly. They are emotional, tending to be interested in spiritual and philosophic matters. They desire to acquire rather than to achieve, and they have a strong sense of objective acquisitiveness.

On the negative side
Imagination becomes illusion; they leap to unconsidered conclusions, believe in unrealities, and chase will-o-the-wisps. Versatility expands to a scattering and wasting of energies; objective desire becomes subjective hope, or wishful thinking. Persuasiveness degenerates into a dominating tendency, which includes a streak of cruelty and fear. Intensity reverts to a destructive force, killing the natural charm of the personality. Emotionalism changes to an impractical, visionary self-indulgence, inducing laziness, thriftlessness, and procrastination.

Balance
Objective concentration, obedience to discipline, the acceptance of limitations, and a simple willingness to work, are the best balancing factors in this picture. The feet of the Taurus SEVENS must be kept firmly on the earth, but at the same time the intensity of their natures must be lightened by laughter and a sense of humour. The Saturn frequency often induces a too great seriousness of viewpoint. They need to cultivate friends of their own sex, to live disciplined, orderly lives, and to develop the habit of sober, practical judgment and discrimination. They need also to accept and fulfil their practical responsibilities from day to day, and to take life as it comes.

Comment
The Tarot document says, of all the SEVENS, that they '*show a force that is like unto a crown but which requireth one capable of wearing it*',

and then adds, with the practical sense so characteristic of all the ten-day cycle descriptions, that the results '*depend upon the action then taken*'. Which puts the matter of success squarely up to the Taurus SEVEN, in his or her choice of what action to take.

When their powerful forces are balanced, their emotions controlled, their activities disciplined and directed with objective intelligence, they have really tremendous potentialities for achievement. Honoré de Balzac is an example of a Taurus SEVEN achieving success through these very qualities. Krishnamurti, the Theosophist author and spiritual leader; Lynn Fontanne, actress; and Margot Fonteyn, great ballet star known for her stamina and self-discipline; Eric Satie, the composer; and Irving Berlin, master of syncopated rhythm, were also born during this cycle, as was that painter of the bizarrely beautiful, the beautifully bizarre, and the 'just plain' (and not so plain) bizarre, Salvador Dali. But the relatively small number of famous Taurus SEVENS on record suggests that these individuals actually do encounter considerable difficulty in gaining the necessary equilibrium to get off to a real start. The dangerous gift of versatility causes many of them, like Stephen Leacock's knight on horseback, to ride furiously in all directions at once, getting nowhere in particular.

The name of the card, 'Success Unfulfilled', suggests that it is not easy for this individual to achieve success, even when it lies, as shown in the picture, directly within his grasp. The golden fruits are ready to gather, but the sturdy farmer leans on his hoe, indulging in a daydream instead of getting to work to pick his apples!

This, it has been found, precisely symbolizes a peculiar laziness that stands between the people born during this period and the very success that they are so well able to attain, and so eager to get. They seem to have a fundamental difficulty in concentrating their efforts on taking the next step, whatever it happens to be. More than this, they often believe sincerely that they have done everything necessary when actually they haven't even started. This is one of their favourite illusions, and illusions are their chief stumbling block.

They have the instinctive charm that pertains to all SEVEN potentials (or Venus frequencies) and which appeals strongly to the opposite sex. They have tremendous vitality, but they are apt to lack fortitude. This, however — as with anything else they really want —

they can develop if they will take the trouble. It has been found that if the desires of the Taurus SEVENS are definitely set in one direction, held there, and well supported by steady, objective, disciplined effort, there is practically nothing in the realm of practical achievement that is beyond their reach.

'Success Unfulfilled'

THE LOVERS.

GEMINI
(May 21 to June 20)

Modern psychology often refers to the conscious and subconscious mind, and to a superconscious mind. This Tarot Key is a picture of the triple structure of human thought and feeling. The conscious mind (the practical thinker) is represented by the Man. The Woman (more receptive, but also indispensable) stands for the subconscious mind, where dreams and images first take shape. The Angel, above, portrays the superconscious realm, the spiritual source of all inspiration, knowledge, wisdom, and love. What this Key is telling you is that only through the combination all three of these within yourself — the Woman, the Man, and the Angel — can you make the best use of your most valuable birthday gift, which is the ability to *think*.

EIGHT of GEMINI

May 21 to 31   (0° to 9°59′ of ♊)

| Potential: EIGHT | Frequency: JUPITER |
| *(Sagacity)* | *(Stability)* |

Basic Quality: AIR
(Mentality)

A quick mind, conservatism, a keen sense of logic, and a desire for justice, are the cornerstones of this personality. The conflict lies between the desire to be fair and the impulse to be kind.

On the positive side
The Gemini EIGHTS are thinkers; their minds are analytical and accurate, observant and clever. They are excellent planners and organizers, willing to work and able to direct the activities of others. They are intensely practical, conscious always of the limitations surrounding them, and never attempting the impossible. They have good judgment, and a gift for accuracy in details. They are orderly, conservative and orthodox, loyal to established customs and tradition. And in spite of all these orderly factors of stability and sagacity, they are warmhearted and generous in their personal relationships, and faithful in friendship. They have a deep sense of personal responsibility.

On the negative side
They are overcritical, narrow-minded, and bigoted. Rather than risk making a mistake they will refrain from action, missing opportunities and restricting their own development. They are obstinate, deaf to suggestions, shortsighted, and often blind to what is going on about them. When negative, the Gemini EIGHTS have trouble with their human relationships, as they tend to be intolerant and impersonal to the point of seeming cold and cruel. They become penny-wise and pound-foolish; they are penurious and ungenerous, too careful of details. Caught in a web of small worries, they lose their vision and their balance.

Balance
Tolerance, gained through clear thinking rather than emotional desire, is one of the best factors of balance for the critical Gemini EIGHTS. Their happiness increases when they learn not to expect too much, at any time, from an imperfect world, and to have faith in the future. They need to cultivate a sense of sportmanship, and practice the art of giving and receiving. And they need to keep their emotions under mental control — letting their heads rule their hearts — without being too strict with themselves. Tempering justice with

mercy is a good idea at all times for any EIGHT of Gemini.

Comment
The quiet, unobtrusive strength of this personality is apt to be misleading; its possessors underestimate its fine qualities, and so do other people. One of the great personalities of history, born during this cycle, gave her name to an age — Queen Victoria. Her name has come to stand for the very qualities most strongly exhibited in this cycle pattern: on the positive side, sterling goodness, clarity of vision, and upright honesty; on the negative side, narrow-minded conventionality, and sometimes a regrettable hypocrisy. The Victorian Age did its best to cover its eyes against the natural phenomena of human life — it was a very prudish period — and it is interesting to note that the figure on the Tarot card is blindfolded.

Expertness in detail is a very real gift with the Gemini EIGHTS. England's 'Old Lady', Queen Victoria, was noted for it; so is the ministry of Norman Vincent Peale, whose advocacy of decent behaviour is again indicative of Gemini EIGHTS. Sam Snead, champion golfer, is famous for his uncanny ability to place his shots precisely. Albrecht Dürer, the German artist, whose marvellous sense of detail and perfection has kept his name, for over five centuries, on the list of immortals in greatness is also a Gemini EIGHT. Sir Arthur Conan Doyle, writer and 'inventor' of Sherlock Holmes, joins the list easily, because of his keen mind and the emphasis he placed on his creation's attention to miniscule clues, and consequent solutions derived therefrom. There are also great literary names gracing this list: Lord Bulwer-Lytton, Rosicrucian and author; Spengler, the philosopher; Ralph Waldo Emerson; and the Good Grey Poet, Walt Whitman. Mesmer, the man who caused the word 'mesmerism' to be brought into our language, is here too; and closer to our own times, John F. Kennedy, Henry Kissinger, and Hubert Humphrey.

Individual analysis has shown that the Gemini EIGHTS are apt to be unduly worried about life in general and their own responsibilities in particular. They are not introverts; they think objectively and clearly, but they have a tendency to restrict their range of opinions and interests, through lack of confidence in themselves and in life generally. This applies, too, to their approach to personal relationships: they are apt to restrict their friendships to one type of person, and to enjoy only one type of entertainment or recreation. The Tarot document credits them with 'patience in detail of study; great care in some things, counterbalanced by equal disorder in others', and states that they 'admire wisdom, yet apply it to small and unworthy objects'.

When well-balanced, they are hospitable and friendly, and, to quote the document again, 'generous, clever, and acute'. In practical affairs, they are especially good at handling the details of money and business; they are adept where statistics are concerned, and they have organizing ability.

The Gemini EIGHTS, in fact, are naturally good citizens, valuable members of a community, well able to handle their lives and to be successful in their undertakings. But, to be happy, they need to cultivate freedom from restriction — to take off the blindfold and let in the sunshine.

'Shortened Force'

NINE of GEMINI

June 1 to 10 (10° to 19°59′ of ♊)

Potential: NINE	Frequency: MARS
(Dependability)	*(Activity)*

Basic Quality: AIR
(Mentality)

Strength, energy, independence, and friendliness are combined in the structure of this personality. The conflict is a battle between the driving desire for practical success and an emotional longing for personal happiness.

On the positive side
The Gemini NINES have executive ability and strong personal force. They have an alert social sense; they are gregarious, hospitable, and very generous, always ready to share what they have with others. They are lovers of action; their energy is infectious and stimulating. They are very intuitive, sensitive, and quick in their reactions and responses. They are deeply affectionate and emotional; personal relations, for them, are vitally important. They are keenly alive to suffering, intensely sympathetic, always eager to help, even at the sacrifice of their own welfare.

On the negative side
They are restless, discontented, and aimless, so eager for change and action that they set no goal, aim for no objective. In their desire for emotional happiness they lose all sense of discrimination in the choice of friends and in their practical activities. Naturally hot-tempered, they become irritable and nervous, unreasonable and headstrong. Naturally adaptable, they are too easily influenced by outside suggestion, and their rapid reactions prevent the considered thinking that would prevent mistakes. Out of balance, they go to extremes. From being delightful, inspiring companions, they become overbearing and officious, always sure that they are right and that everybody else is wrong.

Balance
Self-control, self-discipline, patience, and logical thinking are the

salvation of the Gemini NINES. The Mars frequency always demands self-control, and here, the emotional intensity induced by the NINE potential, in the unstable field of Air, multiplies the need for control in this personality. The adoption of an orderly way of life, the acceptance of conventional limitations, and the building up of self-respect and self-confidence, are all necessary to bring out the best side of these highly-charged natures. Their intuition is keen, but until they link it with reason, it is apt to lead them astray.

Comment

The symbols, the name, and the description of this cycle appear at first view to be rather contradictory, and a bit discouraging. But study and analysis reveal that they are more fortunate than they appear. It seems that picture and symbols are in the nature of a warning to the Gemini NINES to keep the best side of their tempestuous natures uppermost. If they don't, warns the card, they will suffer; if they do, promises the Tarot description, they will be both successful and happy.

The study of many people with birthdays in this cycle has revealed a curious factor relating to the picture on the card, which apparently portrays unhappiness. They possess not only an innate desire to alleviate suffering, but they often have a natural gift for healing. The list of famous people born during the cycle is rather short, and the reason for this seems to be that they are apt to do their work quietly. They are so eager to be helpful and useful that they are careless of fame, and often neglect their own personal welfare and interests. Also, they tend to follow the more unorthodox paths of activity where fame is unlikely.

Emotional self-control seems to be the most necessary discipline for people born during this cycle. The sense of logic and justice that is so strong a feature of the preceding period is lacking in this one. The Mars frequency, in the symbolic spectrum, has the longest wave length (red) and it appears to be the most primitive and uncontrollable of the frequency factors. People born during any Mars cycle have a capacity for destroying their own happiness, and for disturbing the happiness of others — until balance is achieved. When the personality factors are balanced, the Mars frequency induces a friendly, stimulating charm. Broken homes have been restored by the development of self-control in the Mars member of the family! And the most noticeable result of curbing and controlling the emotional forces in this nature has been the improvement of health and happiness in the individual concerned.

This constructive tendency is shown literally by the great architect, Frank Lloyd Wright. Immanuel Velikovsky, the scientist, has reconstructed the history of the earth and its great upheavals. Literary 'giants' have been born during this cycle, among them Alexander Pushkin, Thomas Mann, and Thomas Hardy. However, most of those born in early June pursue their destinies behind the scenes, unknown and unsung. But when they are positive, true to themselves, the world will always be the better for their presence.

Long and careful study of this personality picture, with its puzzling and contradictory symbols, suggests that it should be renamed as a cycle of helpfulness and succor, or just as *sympathy*.

'Despair and Cruelty'

TEN of GEMINI

June 11 to 20   (20° to 29°59′ of ♊)

Potential: TEN   Frequency: SUN
(Persistence)   *(Ambition)*

Basic Quality: AIR
(Mentality)

Determination, fortitude, imagination, and constructive force are all found in this personality. The conflict of the combination lies between the desire to complete the job in hand and the urge to reach out for something bigger.

On the positive side

There is stability and power in this character. The Gemini TENS are dependable, reliable, and honest. They have an innate sense of personal dignity, a love of beauty, a passion for completion and perfection in everything they do. They have an inherent desire for security, and are willing to work for it. They have great tenacity and staying power; they can take a lot of punishment without giving up. They are self-reliant; they have a strong sense of responsibility to family and community. They are very conscientious, and careful of appearances. They are conventional without being narrow-minded; they are tolerant. As always when the Sun frequency is in the picture, they are individualists.

On the negative side

They are exceedingly obstinate, set on following their own will in spite of anything and everything. They refuse to adapt themselves to changing conditions, or to see the danger signals when they appear. Fortitude reverts to foolhardiness, dignity becomes superiority and pride, and the desire for security takes the form of fear, undermining the strength of the character. The cruelty so often found on the negative side of the Sun frequency crops up in this picture, but the Gemini TENS are more apt to be cruel with themselves than with others. There is a masochistic tendency on the wrong side of this personality; they seem to take pleasure in self-inflicted pain, as well as in destroying the happiness of those around them.

Balance

Constant activity, plenty of responsibility, and a cultivation of the gentler qualities of mercy and friendliness, go far to keep the balance on the right side of this rather intense nature. They need also to cultivate the lighter side of life, and not to be too serious, too earnest. They have the natural personal attractiveness of the Sun frequency, and this should be encouraged to show itself in joy and happiness rather than in self-importance. More than all, the Gemini TENS need to develop adaptability. The fixed determination of their wills should be modified and softened, and this can be done successfully through direction of the desires and imagination along pleasant constructive channels.

Comment

After considerable study — preceded by a certain consternation — the symbolic meanings of the picture on the Tarot card belonging to this cycle, and its name, were satisfactorily analyzed. From the first, it was clear that the TEN of Gemini was a cycle of great force, producing strong and positive individuals, many of whom were both charming and successful. So why call it '*Ruin*'? And why the prone figure, transfixed with the ten swords?

It seems that the artist was trying to depict the extraordinary quality of persistent fortitude that is one of the chief characteristics of this personality — you can get them down, but you can't lick them. The Gemini TENS have staying power, and tremendous resistance. They never know when they are beaten, and as they possess very fine positive qualities and considerable personal charm, they have a way of getting what they want in the end. They make good friends, and formidable enemies, because they never acknowledge defeat.

Powerful personalities appear in the cycle's record of famous names, from Nero, who fiddled while Rome burned, to the Duchess of Windsor, who dethroned a king. We also have the person who brought to millions his brilliant characterization of Sherlock Holmes, Basil Rathbone; and Errol Flynn, who animated so many 'larger than life, heroes. The legendary Paul Gauguin, whose romantic life is the stuff that films are made of, is included here. In music, we have Igor Stravinski; in philosophy, Alice Bailey, the Theosophist, and Pascal, who called man 'the thinking reed' — 'reed' because of his frailty, when juxtaposed against nature, and 'thinking' because that was his very grace and his grandeur — to be aware of his circumstances.

In personal studies of people belonging to this cycle, it was found that the charm of the Sun frequency is one of their predominating characteristics. They bear within them the seeds of material success, as every Sun frequency is endowed with 'the gift of acquiring wealth', and the natural ambition of the Gemini TENS is for a position of security. They like to feel themselves well established, with a firm foundations under their feet. Their chief danger lies in over-intensity of purpose, in self-will and egotism, and in pride — which the Tarot document calls 'disdain and insolence'.

'Ruin'

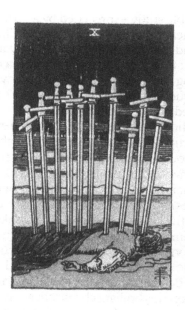

As the balancing factor for every Sun frequency is friendliness, for every TEN potential, adaptability, and for the Air quality, warm-heartedness, it would seem that this fundamental three-way prescription would work out well for the Gemini TENS. Experience has shown that it does; that they are happiest and most successful when they relax their tensions and take life as it comes.

THE CHARIOT.

CANCER
(June 21 to July 21)

The positive, triumphant figure of the Charioteer carries a message of confidence. He is the driver, but needs no reins to drive his steeds, white and black, good and evil. He wears a crown of victory. His belt and apron bear symbols of magical power, attainable only by long and patient effort. There is a popular belief that birthdays in Cancer produce weak and negative characters. The Charioteer disproves this fallacy — his word is *keep on driving!* Your vehicle is provided and equipped. YOU are the driver. His only warning is never to forget that you are driving *two* sphinxes, in harness. One of them is white. The other is black, and will bear constant watching.

TWO of CANCER

June 21 to July 1   (0° to 9°59′ of ♋)

Potential: TWO   Frequency: VENUS
(Initiative)   *(Productivity)*

Basic Quality: WATER
(Flexibility)

Friendliness, intuition, a creative imagination, and strong personal charm, are blended harmoniously in this personality. There is only a slight conflict, taking place between the desire to produce or create, and the restless urge toward change and new things.

On the positive side

The instinctive charm of the Venus frequency, combined with the flexible Water quality, creates here a delightful personality. The Cancer TWOS are gay, pleasure-loving people, affectionate and gregarious, hospitable and generous. They have a keen, intuitive understanding of other people's needs and desires, and they can create a happy atmosphere around them. Like all TWOS, they are ready to start something new at any time, and their quick initiative, plus their active imagination, is one of their best assets. There is a basic sweetness and gentleness in this nature, a kindliness of heart which gives to the personality the quality of genuine friendliness. They have a tendency toward the creative arts, or toward religious mysticism. They are rarely satisfied with mere mental and physical interests; they like to explore the frontiers of the spirit.

On the negative side

They are fickle and changeable, restless and discontented with present conditions. They turn from one activity to another without completing anything, and they distribute their love and affection in too many different directions. Unable to make up their minds through the exercise of logic, they waver from one intuitive idea to another, and when they do manage to come to a decision, they are amazingly obstinate about it. When negative, they are undependable and disloyal, selfish and sensual, lacking discrimination in the choice of friends, environment and undertakings, and they suffer intensely with a deep, emotional unhappiness, as they feel, more keenly than most people, the lack of equilibrium within themselves.

Balance

The intelligent use of intuition is the best way to keep this personality in order. The intuitive power is so keen that if it is encouraged, trained and developed, it will always sound a warning, or indicate the best course to follow. Over-strenuous and impetuous gestures should be avoided. The more easily, quietly, and gracefully the Cancer TWOS approach life, the greater is their chance for happiness and success. They need friends and people about them; alone, they are not happy, and they do not react well to unhappiness. As with all Venus frequencies, a discriminating standard of behaviour and control of the emotions is necessary before the beauty and charm of the personality can be exercised to the best advantage.

Comment
In suggesting to the people born during this period that they develop and train their intuition, it has been found that few individuals have any idea as to how this can be done. The Ten-Day Cycle Formula itself suggests a good procedure, by showing, through the symbols, that *intuition* and *memory* are practically the same function. It has been found, too, that the deliberate effort to develop the habit of accurate remembering, beginning with little things like telephone numbers and shopping lists, will sharpen the tone of the 'still small voice' of intuition so that it can be heard and obeyed.

The Cancer TWOS are found to have a strong creative impulse in their natures, and it seems that these creative functions demand exercise, in some fashion, or their inhibition tends to create a disturbance, like water breaking the bounds of a dam. Any kind of creative activity — from writing a book to making a salad — will help to keep this personality in good balance, functioning right side out. Intuition plays a large part in any creative work, and thus one of the best faculties of this sensitive nature is kept active and alive.

The negative qualities of the cycle show themselves as a rule, in selfishness, in self-indulgence of one kind or another, and often in the simple laziness that is a factor of the Venus frequency. With people born during this cycle there is a tendency toward the more dangerous types of mysticism — on the negative side — psychism, or spiritualism.

When balanced, they are found to have among them many of the most charming, lovable, and attractive people in the world, as well as a number of very brilliant and unusual personalities. Two intuitive scientists have birthdays in this cycle, oddly enough, both on the same day, Alexis Carrel, author of *Man the Unknown*, and Harlan

Stetson, whose work with sunspot cycles has been widely quoted
in the later chapters of this book. The cycle's record includes at least
four remarkable women: Helen Keller, whose conquest of blindness
and deafness made her famous; Pearl Buck, who interpreted for her
readers an alien race; Nancy Fullwood, whose intuitive writings
brought spiritual comfort to thousands of readers; and Ann Morrow
Lindbergh, whose sensitive writings have deeply touched her readers.
Henry VIII belongs in this decante too, as does his contemporary
portrayor, Charles Laughton. Giacomo Puccini, composer of delicate
harmonies and Peter Paul Rubens, painter of the delicate colourings
and sensuous lushness of the female form, were both born here; so
were Luigi Pirandello, playwright, and George Orwell, novelist.

Human problems concern the Cancer TWOS, it seems, more than
the desire for fame. Dr William Mayo, the great humanitarian
surgeon, Theodore Lothrop Stoddard, expert in racial problems, and
E. W. Kemmerer, famous economist, are in this cycle's record. It is
something of a coincidence to find the birthday of the Duke of
Windsor, who gave up a throne for love, with his birthday in this cycle.

'Love'

The title of the Tarot card attributed to the cycle, in the ancient document, is the single word '*love*'.

THREE of CANCER

July 2 to 11   (10° to 19°59' of ♋)

Potential: THREE	Frequency: MERCURY
(Determination)	*(Sagacity)*

Basic Quality: WATER
(Flexibility)

Receptive, sensibility, a quick mind, intensity, and deep human sympathy, are the principal factors in this character. The conflict takes place between the cool judgment of the mind and the warmth of the emotional nature.

On the positive side
This personality possesses the rare combination of a strong intuitive faculty and a keen analytical mind. The Cancer THREES can both feel and think with accuracy, which gives them a dependable, instinctive intelligence that functions easily and naturally. They are by nature pleasure-loving, happy people, capable of great sensuous enjoyment, but having an innate poise and balance, inducing temperance and discrimination. Like all THREES, they have a sympathetic understanding of human sorrow, and feel that they must do something about it. To the world, they are humanitarians; to their friends, they are affectionate, tolerant and generous. They are creative, constructive thinkers, logical and analytical. They have a natural gift of expression through speech, or writing. Their determination, disguised by gentleness, is a strong, almost invulnerable force within their natures.

On the negative side
They allow their emotions and sympathies to get the upper hand, swamping the logical and analytical power of their naturally good minds. Physically, they become self-indulgent, tending toward intemperance in pleasure. They debase their intelligence, using it as craft and cunning, and are capable of resorting to trickery to get what they want. When negative, they are lazy, believing that their

wits will serve in place of positive effort. This indolent tendency brings out the streak of cruelty that is found in the negative side of every THREE potential — a cruelty that is the polar opposite of the positive sympathy. Wrong side out, their normally quick reactions slow down, making them passive, greedy, and selfish.

Balance

A positive, creative approach to life, physical activity, development of the mental faculties, and temperate habits, are the necessary factors of balance to keep the Cancer THREES on the right side of the road. Logical decisions followed by immediate action; the encouragement of ambition toward some practical, concrete goal — these will help to provide the necessary mental discipline for stimulating the fine qualities of this clever, constructive, but oversensitive personality.

Comment

In spite of their natural gift of speech, both in talking and writing, the Cancer THREES, according to the symbols of the cycle, have also the gift of silence. It has been found that this seeming contradiction endows them with the very rare ability to know when to talk and when to keep silent. Sometimes, of course, they go to one extreme or the other — President 'Silent Cal' Coolidge was a typical example. Franz Kafka, whose strange, surrealist stories in which persons do not inform each other of what is going on, but wander dreamlike in a maze of disconnectedness, is a native of this decante. So are Nathaniel Hawthorne, Hermann Hesse, and Marcel Proust. Gustav Mahler, the composer, was also born during this cycle, along with Merv Griffin, Yul Brynner, Louis Armstrong, and Ringo Starr.

There is unquestionable strength in this nature, but it is subtly concealed by the quality of flexibility and by the impersonal viewpoint that is a characteristic of the Mercury frequency. It is a defensive, rather than a fighting force — it is the strength of resistance, not of attack. All THREES are potential reformers, and when they go to extremes on this, they are apt to become fanatics. Usually, however, their sense of logic and rational thinking stop them before it is too late.

They are exceptionally well equipped for clear thinking, and this capacity is best developed in creative and constructive activities. Among people famous for their constructive activities are the

Rockefellers, John D. and his grandson Nelson, whose ability to pick up fortunes fits well with the name of the period's Tarot card, which is 'Abundance'.

This word, of course, has many possible applications, and one of them may well be to the pleasure-loving side of this personality, usually a noticeable feature. Henry VIII is said to have been born in this period, and he loved his food, his drink, and his wives. It has been found, in observing people in all walks of life among the Cancer THREES, that they have a keen sense of enjoyment, an appreciation of the good things of life, which only rarely gets out of bounds, as the logical Mercury frequency comes to the rescue of the self-indignant Water quality.

In the natural equipment of the Cancer THREES there is a real capacity for achievement. The obstacles are laziness, lack of a definite objective — which is a negative tendency in all Water natures — and the danger of allowing the sympathies and emotions to overbalance common sense. But when in balance — which means that the logical mind is commanding and controlling the activities — great things

'Abundance'

can be accomplished by the people born during this cycle. The basic quality of Water gives versatility to their cleverness, and the strength of the THREE potential provides a sound foundation. The Tarot document promises them '*abundance, plenty, good luck and fortune*'.

FOUR of CANCER

July 12 to 21   (20° to 29°59′ of ♋)

Potential: FOUR	Frequency: MOON
(Stability)	*(Adaptability)*

Basic Quality: WATER
(Flexibility)

Serenity, tolerance, optimism, and intuition are the natural gifts of this personality. The conflict lies between the desire for security and the desire for change and expansion.

On the positive side
This is a happy personality, hopeful, poised, and very adaptable. The Cancer FOURS are steady workers, obedient to discipline, willing to conform to the demands of circumstances and make the best of things. They take life as it comes; they are receptive and sensitive to impressions. They are interpreters and synthesizers rather than creators, but they have a highly constructive approach to life — always they prefer to build up rather than to tear down, and always they look forward rather than back. They are intuitive thinkers, but cautious and slow to take action. They are not personally ambitious; they want peace and happiness more than fame and achievement. They are impersonal rather than emotional, but they are sympathetic, forgiving, and generous.

On the negative side
Adaptability becomes passivity, while poise reverts to a static lethargy and laziness. They dream, procrastinate, and wait for things to come to them. They become indolent and self-indulgent. They expend energy on useless and unimportant details; they cling to forlorn hopes. They do not lack courage, but they lack the will to remove obstacles from their way — they want peace at any price. Their impersonality becomes coldness, and their sympathy degenerates

into pity, so that they frequently err on the side of mercy, and lose their perspective in ethical standards. Following intuition rather than logical thinking, they withdraw into a world of illusion, and lose their grip on reality.

Balance

Discrimination, activity, the use of logic, and a policy of common sense and foresight are needed to keep this personality on an even keel. Self-control is called for, both in relation to physical indulgence and to the use of the imagination. The cultivation of a clear mental perspective, sound judgment of people and conditions, and the ability to choose a course of action leading to some worthwhile goal, rather than just drifting, will bring balance to the life of the Cancer FOUR. A determined fight must be waged against over-sensitiveness to impressions, to ideas, and to the actions of other people, and also against over-optimism.

Comment

The establishment of a minority rule is called for in the successful handling of this personality. The stability, sense of order, and common sense of the FOUR potential are apt to be outbalanced by the flexible, intuitive qualities of Water and the Moon frequency. The result of this unbalance is a character having by nature more sweetness than strength, more imagination than determination, and a strong tendency to indulge in wishful thinking.

The positive faculties, however, can be readily developed, as in this gentle personality there is a reservoir of quiet energy, a resilient power of will that comes back again and again to the attack, even after a series of rebuffs that would discourage a less optimistic nature. Extensive study of these apparently passive people has revealed that the personality is like a piece of potter's clay, and can be moulded, by the exercise of will, to any shape that is desired. But in order to be permanent, this moulding must be done by sustained effort on the part of the Cancer FOUR. If it is done by anyone else, the effects disappear overnight.

It has been found that they are apt to be too easily influenced; they take on the colour of their surroundings, like chameleons. They tend to reflect rather than to radiate — as water reflects a blue sky or a cloudy one. For this reason, their selection of associates and of environment is vitally important, as they tend to cling to the things they have even in the face of disappointment and treachery. They are excellent at making the best of a bad job, but they lack the 'punch' to change evil into good, or to get rid of it. Their intense sympathy with other people's suffering causes them, frequently, to be unfair to themselves.

When balanced, they are very charming, productive, and often brilliant. They never lose their gentleness — the most lovable of the three Barrymores was Lionel, who was a Cancer FOUR. Among writers, Isaac Bashevis Singer, Henry David Thoreau, and Marshall McLuhan, have birthdays in this cycle. Among musicians we find Isaac Stern and Van Cliburn; we also find painters Andrew Wyeth, Degas, Marc Chagall, and Rembrandt. Inventor and writer R. Buckminster Fuller belongs here, too. Two great dreamers who integrated their dreams for the good of humanity were Mary Baker Eddy, founder of Christian Science, and the great surgeon Dr Charles Mayo, both born in mid-July. There is in this personality a driving desire for harmony, justice, and human happiness.

'Blended Pleasure'

The flexibility of this character has been found to be at once its greatest charm and its worst danger. The task of bringing it under control without destroying its charm is not an easy one, but the basic symbols of the cycle suggest the best procedure. The picture on the card shows a seated figure, with closed eyes, who only needs to wake up and start moving in order to receive a brimming cup of good fortune straight — as it seems! — from heaven.

LEO
(July 22 to August 22)

This Key is a perfect picture of *energy* — the unnamed power that flows eternally through everything that lives on earth. The Lion, symbol of animal, *physical* force, is obedient to the gentle hands of the Woman. She symbolizes *spiritual* energy, as shown by her white robe and the infinity sign above her head. But the Woman and the Lion are bound together — unified — a chain of roses, symbols of love. They are not two entities, but *one*. Instinctive awareness of this quality of unbroken energy is the special birthday gift from Leo, the Lion, among the three Fire periods of the Zodiac. Note that the Woman, at will, is able either to close the Lion's mouth, quieting him, or to open it, encouraging him to roar. Woman or man, this energy is IN YOU. The choice is yours!

FIVE of LEO

July 22 to August 1   (0° to 9°59′ of ♌)

Potential: FIVE	Frequency: SATURN
(Activity)	*(Intensity)*

Basic Quality: FIRE
(Dynamic Energy)

Determination, personal power, constructive force, and singlemindedness, are the underlying characteristics of this nature. The conflict arises from the fact that the natural factors are all positive, with no modification to relax the tension.

On the positive side
This is a personality of unusually high voltage, with a direct approach to life, great energy, and tireless activity. The Leo FIVES are strenuous workers, and are able to inspire and direct others, either in practical matters or in social life. They have a great capacity for concentrated and continuous effort — they have vitality and staying power, initiative and patience. They are self-starters and self-chargers, running on their own steam. This is a cycle of great power, of dominance and forcefulness, but the Leo FIVES are deeply sympathetic and compassionate to pain and sorrow. They are highly emotional, tending to extremes of affection and loyalty. They are warm-hearted and friendly, always eager to improve conditions and to right wrongs. They have a strong sense of social responsibility.

On the negative side
They are cruel and destructive. Their one desire is for power — over other people and over conditions. They are intolerant and arrogant, ruthless and unprincipled in their actions, unwilling and unable to see any point of view except their own. Leo FIVES, wrong side out, literally turn in upon themselves, like a spring being wound up too tight. They can make themselves and everybody round them utterly miserable, and they become egocentric and introverted, with all their positive personal forces turned inward on their own emotions. They waste their energy in anger, quarrels and ill-considered actions.

Balance
Recognition of their own overpositive tendencies, and the will to soften these by encouraging the friendly side of their natures, is the first step toward equilibrium for the Leo FIVES. They need to learn the art of deliberate relaxation, and to cultivate give-and-take habits in their personal relationships. 'Slow down and take it easy' should be the slogan of every Leo FIVE. Control of the emotions, especially anger and jealousy — and the cultivation of a sense of humour, are

the main keys to balancing this forceful personality. To balance any Saturn frequency, laughter is the best possible medicine.

Comment

In studying the people born during this forceful, fiery cycle, the thing that has been most impressive is their value, as individuals, to the scheme of life. Life, after all, is a battle — there is no escaping from that axiom — and the Leo FIVES are natural born fighters and warriors, both literally and figuratively. The name of the Tarot card is '*Strife*', and the picture shows a group of five athletes, sparring with great energy, but apparently with very little rancor; they really seem to be fighting for the fun of the game, or as if it were the thing to do. Any personality which, like this one, contains in its symbols only positive, masculine, direct forces — the Fire quality, the FIVE potential, and the Saturn frequency — has a fighting spirit that is easily aroused.

The famous names in its record are nearly all of impressive personalities. There is Carl Gustave Jung, master psychologist and philosopher; Henry Ford, I; Aldous Huxley who conquered blindness to become a famous writer; Max Heindel, the Rosicrucian; master talespinners Alexandre Dumas and Herman Melville; Amelia Earhart, the legendary aviatrix; Rasputin, sorcerer and demagogue; and Mick Jagger, ruling rock star, and last but by no means least, the ever-brilliant George Bernard Shaw.

In general, the Leo FIVES are found to be high-strung individuals, who are apt to wind themselves up so tight that their nerves give way under the strain. Their passion for power takes many different forms, and it is often noticeable in family relationships. The Leo FIVE will be the dominant personality in the house, for good or ill according to the degree of balance in the individual, and also according to the strength or weakness in the surrounding characters. The gentler natures stand no chance against a Leo FIVE — the power complex mows them down and tramples on them, quite often with the best intentions in the world, and with gestures that are apparently considerate and kindly, but are actually quite the reverse.

Because they are so positive, with all the weight on one side of the scale, the Leo FIVE usually has to make a deliberate effort to relax at regular intervals, to adjust, as it were, to the normal human ebb and flow, which is constantly shifting from one end of the pole to the other. Adjustment and adaptability do not come easily to this nature, because of its tendency toward a fixed point of view. Like Alice in Wonderland, they put their minds so hard on a point that the point sticks through. Perhaps more than any other group in the pattern, the Leo FIVES need to learn the simple art of living in a world of give-and-take, and to accept life as it comes. When they do this, they can be, as already suggested, very valuable individuals, for in the bigger issues of life they will fight to the last ditch for any cause they set their hearts upon.

'Strife'

SIX of LEO

August 2 to 11   (10° to 19°59′ of ♌)

Potential: SIX	Frequency: JUPITER
(Ambition)	*(Stability)*

Basic Quality: FIRE
(Dynamic Energy)

Dignity, joviality, idealism, and an indomitable will make up the structure of this personality. There is only a slight conflict, which comes up between the desire to be generous and the desire to be absolutely fair.

On the positive side
This nature is extraordinarily well balanced. The Leo SIXES have a sense of personal power, self-confidence, and poise. They are vital and dynamic, exerting a strong influence over people and conditions. They have a strong sense of justice; their minds are orderly; they are loyal to conventions and tradition. They are idealistic rather than practical, but they have great energy and endurance. Desiring peace above everything else, they are willing to fight for it; desiring beauty and perfection in all things, they willing to work for what they want. In personal relationships they are warmhearted and passionately loyal. They have great personal charm, in addition to their instinctive and unfailing dignity. The Leo SIX is a natural leader, well equipped to occupy positions of importance and responsibility.

On the negative side
They are intolerant, overbearing, and self-centred. Everything is sacrificed to their ambitions, even their friends and those they love. They are proud, sensitive to criticism, narrow-minded and bigoted. Their generosity does not, as is often the case, expand into extravagance on the negative side — it contracts into stinginess and fear of loss. Their dignity becomes standoffishness, and their only friendliness is patronage. With such strong positive qualities, their wrong-side-out expression is equally powerful. The negative Leo SIX can be most unhappy, and can bring great unhappiness to others.

Balance
Friendliness, and the tempering of justice with mercy, are the best balancing factors of the Leo SIX. When the kindly side of the SIX potential is encouraged, it has the same general effect as sunshine, warming and tempering the atmosphere. Tolerance and adaptability, sincerity and good sportmanship at all times, help considerably toward keeping the Leo SIXES right side out. The magnetic charm of their personality needs all its natural dignity, plus a little extra

gentleness, in order to function at its best.

Comment

The egotism of the Leo SIXES seems to have some quality of magic about it, as if the charm of the personality tends to make it a virtue rather than a fault. They take the centre of the stage — and keep it — with such grace and confidence that they are usually allowed to get away with it. As a matter of fact, this egotism is, in itself, a valuable quality, for it is one of the necessary personal ingredients of the leader, and the Leo SIXES have an innate capacity for leadership.

Their problem, of course, is to use this dominant quality constructively. When they are not in positions of authority, their frustrated sense of superiority is apt to take itself out in treading on other people's toes. It has been found that while this personality can attract more love and loyalty than almost any other in the pattern, it can also attract more bitter hatred, jealousy and dislike. There is tremendous force and power in their natures — either for good or evil.

Tremendous workers and idealists like Arthur Goldberg, former U.S. representative to the United Nations; Herbert Hoover, who was well respected for the work he did with poor people before he became president; and Mata Hari, who worked hard for her country, in her own way — all are famous SIXES. So are poets Shelley and Alfred Lord Tennyson; novelist Guy de Maupassant; film director John Huston; and that timeless vital actress, Lucille Ball.

This cycle is the second 'peak period' of the wave of the solar year. It has not been found to produce a very high average of famous names, but those in the list are of influential, powerful people, noted for their vitality, ability, charm, and dignity. The emotional quality of Fire gives to the Leo SIXES a greater dynamic force than any of the other peak groups, but they are less clever and intelligent than the Aquarius SIXES, who occupy the peak of famous births. The Jupiter frequency, it seems, gives a logical mind, but not the quick, brilliant mentality of the Mercury frequency. All the SIXES, as noted, are natural egotists, but the Leo SIXES, because of the sense of justice inherent in the Jupiter frequency, are more inclined toward kindness and away from cruelty than any of the others. In dealing with them, it has been found, the best way of approach is through the heart, not the head. They always want to be top dog, and the only way to get them to yield a point is by rousing their emotions — love or hate, pity or loyalty, or (on the negative side) jealousy. There is no use appealing to their reason, as there, they are convinced, they are quite unassailable.

They love beauty, and hate disorder and ugliness. Their desire is for perfection and completion, and they are very hard to satisfy. The Leo SIXES are not easy to live with, to work with, or to understand, but analysis of study of them has shown very clearly that they carry the seeds of greatness within their natures, and this is one of the cycles from which may come those individuals most needed by a chaotic world — *leaders*, just and honourable, strong and kind, willing to accept and to fulfill responsibility.

'Victory'

SEVEN of LEO

August 12 to 22   (20° to 29°59′ of ♌)

Potential: SEVEN	Frequency: MARS
(Versatility)	*(Activity)*

Basic Quality: FIRE
(Dynamic Energy)

Courage, resourcefulness, imagination, and intensity are the vital components of this personality. The conflict takes place between the desire for supremacy, which implies concentration, and the tendency to scatter, or diversify the interests.

On the positive side
The Leo SEVENS are dominant, vital people, always ready for action, adventure — or a battle. They are energetic and enthusiastic; tireless themselves, they are capable of inspiring others to work with them and for them. They have great charm, especially for the opposite sex. They are emotional, highly charged, and passionate in their personal affections. Their imaginations are vivid and creative; they tend to dramatize everything in life, from petty details to great enterprises. They have the ability for intense concentration, and when positive, they are entirely without fear. Under pressure, they exhibit great fortitude, and resourcefulness is one of their most valuable assets.

On the negative side
They are fighters, taking, at all times, the opposition or the defensive. They are quarrelsome, proud, touchy, and obstinate. They lack the ability to co-operate with others; they desire always to dominate and direct. Their resourcefulness become mere excitability and impetuosity; they rush into action without considering the consequences. Wrong side out, they are apt to be cruel in personal relationships, especially where the emotions are involved. Their versatility leads them to scatter their energies so widely that the effort to concentrate on a number of things at the same time destroys their mental balance, making them highly irritable, nervous, and undependable. It is difficult for them to co-ordinate their energies.

Balance
Self-control, first, last and all the time, is the main balancing factor for the Leo SEVEN. Discipline is demanded always by both the Mars frequency and the SEVEN potential, and here, both of these are found in combination, doubling the need. Self-discipline in matters of daily living, order and regularity in routine, obedience to conventions, and the strictest honesty in all human relationships are essential for

equilibrating the powerful forces of this nature. The emotions — anger, hatred, jealousy — call for constant curbing, as they have, in this combination, an explosive quality that is not easy to handle. For practical success, concentration on one thing at a time is the key, and for personal happiness — again, self-control.

Comment

The Leo SEVENS would seem, at first glance, to have everything their own way. But it has been found that they are rather like a man with a team of fiery horses, no whip, and only slender ribbons for reins. The horses have to be driven and controlled by sheer will — so the problem of this cycle is contained in that hoary proverb to the effect that he who will conquer the world must first conquer himself. And for the Leo SEVENS, this undertaking is a little harder than usual, because their nervous systems are, as it were, supercharged with electricity. The Tarot credits them with '*boldness, rashness, violence, desire, generosity*', adding, shrewdly enough, that their success depends on '*dignity*'.

Their versatility is of an unusual type. Not only can they do a surprising number of different things, but they do them all astonishingly well, apparently without training or preparation. But the net result of this magic is rather likely to be that the roof is placed on an edifice built without foundations, so that the first storm blows it down. The imagination of the Leo SEVENS knows no bounds. They have to learn, and to practice, the art of doing one thing at a time, and of completing one job before they start the next one. The average Leo SEVEN leaves a trail of unfinished business.

Most famous of them is Napoleon Bonaparte. He is a perfect example of the cycle's great possibilities, and his ultimate failure came from the characteristic inability of his personality to see himself in any role but that of a conqueror, and thus to forget, or to ignore, practical caution. Mme. H. P. Blavatsky, founder of the Theosophical Society, who almost single-handedly brought the wisdom of the East to the western world and Sri Aurobindo, great Indian mystic, poet, and author, were born during this cycle. Others include: the great novelist John Galsworthy; director of larger than life epics Cecil B. DeMille; director and master of suspense Alfred Hitchcock; notorious revolutionist Fidel Castro; British archaeologist, adventurer, and author T. E. Lawrence (Lawrence of Arabia); and actor Robert Redford.

The instability of the cycle probably accounts for its low average of famous names, but in everyday life many of the more lively and exciting people one meets turn out to be Leo SEVENS. They are found, under analysis, to be unhappy only when their vision is greater than their actual capacities, or because they are so unwilling to take one step at a time. They want to reach the top in a single jump. They can *see* themselves doing it — and so, they argue, why bother about the laws of gravitation?

They take their knocks well, however, and no one of them has yet been found to be discouraged for longer than a few hours. They have amazing powers of recuperation, and are always ready to try again. The one thing they really want is the same thing Napoleon wanted — in some fashion or other to conquer the world. And, once they can conquer the fiery forces of their own natures, there is no reason

'Valor'

why they cannot do it, especially if they take that one little tip from the Tarot and retain, at all times, their personal dignity.

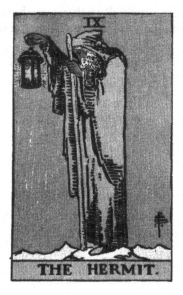

VIRGO
(August 23 to September 22)

The beautiful, silent figure of the Hermit appears to be alone, aloof from the cares and troubles of the world below. In reality, he is so concerned with the troubles of humanity — arising, as he has learned on his own climb to the mountain top — from ignorance and folly, that he has paused to light the way for those who follow him. All three Virgo Decanates are equipped with a strong sense of responsibility to others, each in a different direction, but all heading toward one goal — the goal already reached by the Hermit. He holds the lantern high to light YOUR way, and he waits, with infinite patience, for you to catch up with him.

EIGHT of VIRGO

August 23 to September 1   (0° to 9°59′ of ♍)

Potential: EIGHT	Frequency: SUN
(Sagacity)	*(Ambition)*

Basic Quality: EARTH
(Practical Sense)

Caution, efficiency, skill in details, and an active imagination are the chief factors in this character. The conflict lies between the urge of ambition and the restriction of the prudent, analytical mind.

On the positive side
This is a rational, dependable personality, capable of developing a high degree of skill in any type of work that demands attention to facts or details. The Virgo EIGHTS are meticulous workers; they are logical, constructive thinkers, having a keen sense of responsibility. They finish anything they start, and, in spite of their active imaginations, they are extremely practical and efficient. They like to follow tradition and convention, rather than to blaze new trails, but they are fundamentally courageous. They have good mental ability, patience, and tolerance. They are loyal and affectionate, orderly and trustworthy. Their emotions are under excellent control, and they have a quiet, magnetic personal charm.

On the negative side
They are overcautious, narrow-minded and prudish, unwilling to take a step until they have planned for every imaginable emergency. They waste energy on small and unimportant things, thus losing perspective and vision. They are penny-wise and pound-foolish, avaricious, and miserly. They are intolerant, critical of the behaviour and morals of other people. They limit their activities to a restricted range, and stick to their regular habits with an almost religious intensity, discouraging adventures even of the mind, thus inhibiting their mental development and losing all sense of initiative and enterprise.

Balance
A sympathetic viewpoint, patience with other people's inefficiencies and weaknesses, plus the keeping alive of personal ambition and a broad vision — these are the needed balancing factors for the Virgo EIGHT. The warmth of the Sun frequency should be developed and encouraged to equilibrate the impersonal coolness of the EIGHT potential and the practical, detail-conscious quality of Earth. A sense of adventure, adaptability, and tolerance, are the positive attributes

in this nature that should be kept in the forefront. And always the Virgo EIGHT should guard against the type of blindness that 'can't see the wood for the trees'.

Comment

In this cycle, it seems that the ambition and charm of the Sun frequency is somewhat hampered by the combination of a sagacious EIGHT potential and the practical quality of Earth. A psychologist, in such a case, would expect to find inhibitions and repressions, and the results of personal analysis have shown that people born during this period are sometimes given to indulging in the most familiar of the 'complexes' — a sense of inferiority. This lack of confidence in themselves is in such direct contradiction to the positive expression of any Sun frequency that it throws the personality of the Virgo EIGHT out of balance.

The restoration of self-respect, which can be accomplished by emphasizing the value of the positive qualities — the ability, skill, and trustworthiness of the nature — has been found to be constructive procedure for the Virgo EIGHTS. They need to realize that the practical sense and prudence that is natural to them make its possessors highly desirable people under almost any circumstances in life.

Probably because of the inhibited ambitions and undue modesty there is a rather short available list of famous names in the cycle's record. However, we do find Aubrey Beardsley, the great *fin-de-siècle* portrayer of exquisite decadence; Theodore Dreiser, whose painstaking construction of plot and scene is consistent with Virgo EIGHT, and Leonard Bernstein, brilliant composer-conductor. We also note here the great universal genius Johann von Goethe, poet, philosopher, playwright, novelist, botanist, and scientist. The Tarot document credits them with '*skill, prudence, and cunning*'.

They are rarely given to self-indulgence, and their tendency is to take life rather seriously and earnestly. While they possess, through the Sun frequency, an innate appreciation of beauty and pleasure, their practical, rational qualities are so much in the ascendancy that they are apt to forget how to play. The EIGHT potential carries with it, as a rule, an acceptance of restriction which can be rather destructive to happiness as well as to ambition. While they are usually happiest and most successful when aiming at a goal that is material and concrete, rather than idealistic, they need to remember to keep their dreams alive, and above all to keep their desires constantly reaching out for greater achievement, beyond the limits of their present picture. Expansion of activities, relationships, and vision, is the key to the best development of the Virgo EIGHTS.

This is one of the cycles to which the Tarot document assigns the enviable ability of '*acquiring wealth*'. It has been found that many of the Virgo EIGHTS have a real capacity for making money, and attracting it, and also that they seem to be exceedingly honest in their handling of financial matters. And there is no doubt that when they remember not to take life too seriously, they can be as charming as they are honest.

'Prudence'

NINE of VIRGO

Sepetmber 2 to 11   (10° to 19°59′ of ♍)

Potential: NINE   Frequency: VENUS
(Dependability)   *(Productivity)*

Basic Quality: EARTH
(Practical Sense)

Independence, intuition, creative thinking, and instinctive
personal charm are the main components of this personality.
The conflict takes place between the desire for practical
achievement and the emotional urge toward self-indulgence.

On the positive side
The Virgo NINES are creative and imaginative, with keen intuition,
practical ability, and the will to make a dream come true in concrete
form. They have great personal attraction, and a considerable
capacity for physical pleasures. They are given to extremes of intense
activity and equally intense lethargy — they either work, or loaf,
completely. They are highly sensitive, quick to react and respond
to changing conditions, but they are also very independent, self-
contained, and shrewd. They have executive and organizing ability,
with a keen instinctive understanding of other people's needs and
desires. They are emotional, affectionate, and very loyal.

On the negative side
The NINE potential and the Venus frequency, both being normally
on the negative side of the field, tend to intensify the negative
expression of these individuals. Wrong side out, they are lazy,
unambitious, and self-indulgent. They utilize their intuition to jump
to conclusions, in the effort to avoid real work, and they turn their
understanding of people to use in getting what they want, regardless
of consequences. When negative, the Virgo NINES are apt to be
shiftless, bad-tempered, unhappy people, with all their ability and
charm going to waste with a curious and almost tragic intensity. They
become covetous and jealous, and are apt to lose their sense of ethical
responsibility.

Balance
General self-control, and steady, disciplined activity, are excellent balancing factors for the Virgo NINES. While the intuition should be encouraged and developed, discrimination in its use is desirable and necessary; it must be a practical working tool and not an emotional indulgence. The desires and emotions, in this personality, are very powerful, requiring a tight rein and firm handling in order to keep the personality positive, and to provide constructive channels of activity for its creative forces.

Comment
Concerning all cycles with a Venus frequency, any comment made from a purely logical point of view is sure to be unsatisfactory. The Venus frequency in itself is an emotional, feminine, unstable force, difficult to control and hard to put to really constructive use. Its best asset is its instinctive charm, which is based on what is called sex appeal — currently *oomph* — and so defies analysis. It can only be felt; it can never be understood or analyzed.

With the Virgo NINES, it seems, this delightful quality is very strong, and it has been interesting to find that while the period produces many attractive individuals, its list of famous names is below the average. This may be because there is, among the cycle's symbols, no suggestion whatever of ambition or the desire for power. What this personality wants is to create, to produce, to bring forth fruit of one kind or another. The name of the card is '*Material Gain*', and it has been found that when they are well balanced, the Virgo NINES are apt to be fortunate in financial matters, so that the harvest is a good one. So it is not surprising that we find here J. P. Morgan, a name practically synonymous with wealth. Wealth, however, is not the only goal for the creative perseverance of these personalities. There is also an intensity in the force of the Venus frequency which, linked with the Earth quality, as it is here, gives great vitality to the achievements of this personality. Grandma Moses is an example of this vitality: the literary giant Leo Tolstoy is another. Many of the Virgo NINES tend to take the troubles of the human family deeply to heart. It is this attention to such details that enables great comic actors Peter Sellers and Sid Caesar to portray so accurately the strange frailties of their fellow men. Many of Virgo NINES feel a similar emotion, but failing to find an outlet for its expression, turn it inward and work it off in some form of emotional indulgence. It seems that finding a way of using the creative intensity of their natures is one of the most important problems for the Virgo NINES. David Seabury, writer and psychologist, whose interest is in the troubles of the individual human being, was born during this cycle.

As well as the creative force, there is in this personality an impatience with superficial things and a desire for a fundamental basis in life. In general, the Virgo NINES are found to be home-loving and affectionate, and they are happiest when living a normal, busy, domesticated life. While they can be highly sophisticated, there is a primitive streak in their structure, which demands the simple things rather than the complications of modern civilization. Perhaps more than any other individuals in the pattern, the Virgo NINES need to live close to nature, rather than in cities.

'Material Gain'

TEN of VIRGO

September 12 to 22   (20° to 29°59′ of ♍)

Potential: TEN   Frequency: MERCURY
(Persistence)   *(Sagacity)*

Basic Quality: EARTH
(Practical Sense)

Determination, intelligence, integrity, and dependability are the outstanding factors in this character. The conflict lies between the quick reactions of the mind and the slower reactions of the emotions.

On the positive side
There is great strength and ability in this personality. The sturdy persistence of the TEN potential, combined with the logic and cleverness of the Mercury frequency, working in the practical field of Earth, together suggest a broad capacity for achievement. The Virgo TENS are natural extroverts; they think objectively. Their actions are always directed toward a concrete result or goal. They have keen analytical minds, and with their intellectual activity they combine an instinctive sagacity, a mental sensibility, which endows them with discrimination. They are industrious, painstaking workers, always practical, and their natural trend is toward the establishing of a sound foundation in their lives. They want security, order, and a sense of rightness in all their actions and relationships.

On the negative side
They are impersonal and selfish, wrapped up in their material ambitions to the exclusion of everything else. They see nothing in life but the single objective of getting ahead in a practical way, gaining possessions and attaining a position of security. They are heartless, sometimes cruel, very critical of other people, impatient and ruthless. Their sensibility turns to oversensitiveness and irritability. Wrong side out, the Virgo TENS can be most unhappy, and also destroy the happiness of others. Their emotions are a problem, as they do not flow easily, and so tend to choke up the streams of vitality and activity.

Balance

Exercise of the natural discrimination is a great safeguard against becoming negative. With the Mercury frequency, the mind is always a more dependable tool than the intuition or emotions. Also, the Virgo TENS are happier and better when they do not concentrate with too much intensity on practical problems. When negative, they worry, becoming overpessimistic and fearful of losing what they have. But, if logic and clear thinking are kept in the ascendancy, the emotions keep their proper place in the picture, making possible both personal happiness and practical achievement.

Comment

More than twice as many famous names appear in the list of Virgo TENS as in the preceding cycle, suggesting, perhaps, that the Mercury frequency is a useful asset in the battle for the high places. The peak-of-fame cycle, the Aquarius SIX, has also a Mercury frequency, and this tends to support the conventional idea that intelligence is the first necessity in real achievement. Mercury, in all systems of symbolism, is used as an emblem of the mind and the intellect, and the accuracy of its various positions in the Formula are borne out by the evidence of the individuals born during those cycles. They turn out, in all cases, to be clever people, and often they are famous and powerful as well.

The roll of fame bristles with distinguished names. Writers H. G. Wells, John Knowles, William Golding, and Ken Kesey. In acting, Peter Falk, and such fascinating actresses as Anne Bancroft, Greta Garbo, Sophia Loren, and Lauren Bacall. Agnes de Mille, choreographer, is on the list, as well as Samuel Johnson, English author, critic, and first lexicographer of the English language, who lent his name to an age of literature; and Dr Ellsworth Huntington of Yale, author of *Season of Birth*, the man who first established the scientific validity of birthdate significance.

In personal analysis and contracts, it has been found that the psychological conflict within the Virgo TENS is a considerable one. It can create a nervous upset and disturbance out of all proportion to the reality. When the mental forces are dominant in a practical personality, the emotional forces are necessarily recessive — and it is usually the underdogs who are unmanageable and make trouble.

With these individuals, the tendency to irritability and anger, which arises from the insulation, or damming-up, of the emotions, can be readily controlled once its cause is recognized.

When, instead of following the negative tendency to bottle them up, the simple emotions of love and friendliness are encouraged to flow freely, and to be expressed in words, actions, and gestures, the Virgo TENS will both give and receive much greater happiness in all personal relationships. Not only in their personal lives, but in their practical business problems, they find it helpful to keep free from tensions and strain. It seems that they are over-critical of themselves as well as of others; their tendency is to drive themselves too hard for too long periods at a stretch, without stopping to relax. And a single glance at the recorded achievement of the cycle, in the names listed above, will assure the Virgo TENS that the attainment of balance, for them, is likely to be well worth the effort it entails.

'Wealth'

LIBRA

(September 23 to October 22)

This Key carries no threat of sin and punishment, despite the sword and scales held so firmly by the lady on her throne. Unlike most representations of Justice, she wears no blindfold. She wears, instead, a jewelled crown, and a rich robe of red and green. Her message is clearly contained in a single word — *equilibrium*. She is the symbol of personal poise and balance, particularly in the face of problems calling for sudden decision. She asks you to make certain that you understand *both* sides of any conflict, and *all* sides of any complex situation, before decision and action. The two pillars between which she sits symbolize *severity* and *Mercy*. She brings into play, in YOU, this needed balance for continued success and happiness.

TWO OF LIBRA

September 23 to October 2   (0° to 9°59′ of ♎)

Potential: TWO	Frequency: MOON
(Initiative)	*(Adaptability)*

Basic Quality: AIR
(Mentality)

A flexible mind, intuition, compliance, and human understanding, are the fundamental qualities of this nature. The conflict lies between the desire to follow the promptings of intuition and the tendency to yield to outside opinion.

On the positive side

This personality is gifted with clear vision, quick mental reactions, intuitive understanding of people and conditions. The Libra TWOS are poised, yet flexible and yielding. They are calm, impersonal, and independent, but affectionate and loyal to family ties. They have a keen publicity sense; they know what people want and how to give it to them. They have excellent memories, and considerable creative ability. They are able to adjust themselves to extreme changes of circumstances and conditions, with ease and charm. They are natural peacemakers, disliking strife of any kind, and they can create a happy, contented atmosphere around them. They are very generous, sympathetic, and quick to respond to emotion.

On the negative side

They are restless, unstable, uncertain as to their objectives. They follow 'hunches' without stopping to judge them as good or evil. They are blown by the winds of indecision, unable to make up their minds about anything. They are too easily influenced by people of more positive natures, and they fail to set up and adhere to a set of standards of their own. They start things, and fail to finish them — wrong side out, the Libra TWOS lack the integrative force necessary to complete any undertaking. Their tendency is to drift, like a ship without a rudder; they procrastinate, hesitate, and doubt their own abilities. When negative, they suffer from an intense, intangible unhappiness.

Balance

The recognition and understanding of their own inner uncertainties is the first step toward balance for the Libra TWOS. The development of mental independence, so that they are not swayed by other people's opinions, and can follow their own intuitive decisions without hesitation, is their most important job in life. Activity and change, even in small things, are good medicine for any Moon frequency, and particularly for this one. It is never advisable for the Libra TWOS to indulge in severe self-discipline, remorse, or over-strenuous efforts along one line of action. They accomplish a better balance by yielding to their own instinctive ebb and flow of energy.

Comment

This is perhaps the most impressionable of all the personalities in the pattern — that is, the Libra TWOS are more quickly receptive to ideas, emotions, and intangible sensations, than most of the rest of us. Their intuition is so keen that it is almost like an extra sense, and their memories are so good that the unhappy recollections, with them, are apt to live on long after they should have been forgotten.

They swing, like pendulums, from one extreme to the other, and while they earnestly desire peace, or equilibrium, in their lives, they find it difficult of attainment. The balance of the Libra TWOS is very delicate — like a jeweller's scale, a grain of sand will tip it one way or the other. And curiously, it has appeared that while the Libra TWOS find it hard to come to a decision, to make up their minds, they can be, once they *have* decided, unbelievably obstinate. It almost seems as if they had dual personalities, the one being too yielding, the other hard and stubborn. And they change from one to the other with disconcerting abruptness.

Inutition being such an outstanding factor of the personality, it is interesting to find that among the famous birthdays in the cycle's record is that of Dr J. B. Rhine, of Duke University, whose researches in Extra-Sensory-Perception, or telepathy, roused universal public interest. Three famous mystics are in the list: Annie Besant, Theosophical leader; Nicholas Roerich, painter of Tibetan gods and spirits; and Cyril Scott, composer and writer on the occult significance of music. Mahatma Gandhi, Indian religious and social leader, was born in this cycle, as well. Groucho Marx is a Libra TWO; and another is Al Capp. Vladimir Horowitz, the great classical pianist, and Marc Edmond Jones, astrologer, expand the list. Among writers we have F. Scott Fitzgerald, Graham Greene, and William Faulkner.

The Tarot document devotes more space then usual to these personalities, and the main point of its argument is the basic instability of the personality. It says, in part; 'Contradictory characters in the same nature; truth and untruth; sorrow and sympathy; sometimes selfish and sometimes unselfish'.

This suggests that for these individuals, even more than is generally the case, a balancing of the personal factors is essential to happiness and success in life. It has been found that intense concentration on a single subject, a single objective or mode of life, is not the best procedure for the Libra TWOS. They seem to need change and variety as a flower needs sunlight, and when they fail to get it, they are apt to take some extreme form of escape — over-indulgence in pleasure, especially eating and drinking, or mental adventurings into the psychic and supernatural. The latter type of escape is especially destructive for the Libra TWOS, because of their great sensibility to subtle, or imaginary, impressions.

When balanced, they are extremely charming, very popular — because of their ready sympathy and quick responses — and there is a sweetness in their natures that is generally found with the Moon frequency and the TWO potential. They are particularly well equipped to bring people harmoniously together, and for the interpretation of ideas for general, public understanding.

'Peace Restored'

THREE of LIBRA

| October 3 to 12 | (10° to 19°59′ of ♎) |

| Potential: THREE | Frequency: SATURN |
| *(Determination)* | *(Intensity)* |

Basic Quality: AIR
(Mentality)

Perseverance, dependability, seriousness, and constructive force are the pillars of this character. There is practically no conflict — if any, it arises from the overpositive intensity of the nature.

On the positive side
This is a character in which strength, integrity, and power are combined with a deep understanding of human sorrow. The Libra THREES have a passionate desire to alleviate suffering, and to improve the conditions of human life — whatever may be the individual's sphere of activity: the home, the office, the community, or the nation. They have good administrative ability; they are enterprising, constructive, tireless workers. They are never idle; always there is some objective toward which they are heading, from childhood to old age. They have tremendous vitality, and great resistance; their recuperative powers are remarkable. When positive, their tolerance of the weaknesses of others is as great as their own basic strength. They are natural humanitarians.

On the negative side
They are fanatics, so much in earnest about their own particular theories of progress that nobody else can possibly be right about anything. When negative, their intensity of purpose can follow a destructive course with all the perseverance of their powerful natures — which, when positive, are so vitally constructive. Wrong side out, the Libra THREES can create much trouble for themselves and for everybody round them. They are impervious to outside opinion, deaf to suggestion or criticism. They become critical, harsh, and cruel, and suffer intensely, themselves, in doing so. They are dogmatic and officious, determined to force their own wills on everybody within their sphere of influence.

Balance

For every Saturn frequency, especially when doubled with the THREE potential, whose forces are similar, the best and only balance is a sense of humour. Laughter is the equilibrating magic to release and relax the terrific intensity of this personality. The deep human sympathy that is at the heart of the Libra THREES can follow its kindly, natural course when balanced by laughter and humour, and when this balance is attained, the true greatness of the character shines through. They need, as well, to use their naturally good intellectual forces, and cultivate the art of logical thinking, so as to avoid being carried away by a fanatical impulse or idea.

Comment

The extraordinary force of this personality does not include the fire of ambition, and experience has shown that some of its most interesting examples are people the world will never hear of, as they do their work behind the scenes rather than out in front. And the very intensity of the Libra THREES is apt to defeat its own purpose by its too great seriousness, which causes it to turn in upon tself, and, as it were, stall its own engine.

But the record shows some names that fit the picture well. Niels Bohr, Danish physicist and Nobel prize winner; writers Helen MacInnes, Cervantes, Thomas Wolfe, and Gore Vidal; Giuseppe Verdi, Italian opera composer; Thelonious Monk, composer-pianist; Helen Hayes, actress; Aleister Crowley, occultist and eccentric; and John Lennon, musician and former Beatle.

On the negative side, there is an unquestionably destructive force in the nature of the Libra THREES. The mythological legends report of Saturn that he 'ate his own children', thereby destroying the very thing he wanted to create. Observation of individuals born during this positive, fanatical cycle has suggested that some of the tendencies attributed, symbolically, to the ancient god, have a way of appearing in his modern representatives. By the very force of their own intensity they seem to repel, or destroy, instead of attracting to them, the very things they want most in life.

But there can be no doubt, from the symbols as well as from the evidence of the people born during this period, and their approach to life, that the positive expression of this personality is a strong force

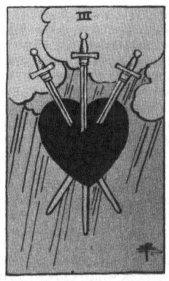

for good, and functions naturally on the constructive side, not the destructive — particularly when its individuals remember not to take life too seriously.

The Tarot document lists their strong and weak points without mercy; it credits them on the one hand with 'faithfulness in promises, honesty in money transactions', and on the other it accuses them of 'mischief-making, sorrow and tears, sowing of discord and strife'. Experience has shown that the more strength there is on the positive side of a powerful personality, the greater will be the power of the negative side. And, as can be seen, the Libra THREES are among the most powerful, forceful personalities in the pattern — for good, or evil, as they choose.

FOUR of LIBRA

October 13 to 22   (20° to 29°59′ of ♎)

Potential: FOUR   Frequency: JUPITER
(Stability)   *(Stability)*

Basic Quality: AIR
(Mentality)

A sense of justice, a logical mind, reliability, and generosity are the fundamentals in this character. The conflict is only a slight one; it lies between the desire to be absolutely fair and the instinct toward mercy and kindness.

On the positive side
The Libra FOURS are orderly, conventional, obedient to discipline and tradition, but their sense of duty is agreeably modified by a keen appreciation of pleasure and the ability to enjoy life. They have naturally good self-control, but they also have a joviality of nature that gives them great personal charm. They are even more dependable than the FOURS — anything they start, they finish, and their standards of perfection are high. They have creative and constructive ability. They are clear, logical and analytical thinkers, and their mental responses are quick and accurate. They are restful, companionable, and they have a fine sense of sportsmanship. They are apt to be popular and highly respected, especially when they follow established, traditional lines of life and activity.

On the negative side
They are overcritical, faultfinding, and hard to please. Wrong side out, they are self-indulgent, selfish and proud, easily hurt and sensitive to criticism. They are very obstinate, narrow-minded to the point of bigotry, and their sense of logic is put to use in captious argument, in which they will never yield an inch. Their sense of justice, when negative, leans to the side of severity and cruelty — mercy is out of the picture. The negative Libra FOURS are curiously sulky; when angry or annoyed, they take refuge in a sullen silence, and this repression is a disturbing element in their lives, both psychologically and physically. They antagonize people, and shut themselves away from normal life.

Balance
An intelligently optimistic viewpoint is the mental safeguard of the Libra FOURS. They are better able than most people to see all sides of any question, and they can choose, if they will, the sunny side rather than the gloomy one. Logic, for them, is a much more successful weapon than emotion or imagination. A consistent

attitude of dignity, too, is necessary to these individuals; they have to retain their natural poise at all times, as it is an integral part of their general equilibrium. Balance, for the Libra FOURS, is not nearly so difficult a problem as it is for many other personalities. They can achieve it, as it were, instinctively.

Comment

If anyone were planning to choose, from the Ten-Day Cycle Formula alone, the best person to constitute a one-man — or one-woman — court of justice — a positive, balanced Libra FOUR would be the best choice. The combination of honesty, fairness, human understanding, and the ability to analyze a situation from all angles, is found to a surprising degree in the people born during this cycle. If Diogenes, with his lantern, had found a Libra FOUR, his story might have been a happier one.

The two sides of this personality — gloomy and cheerful — are well illustrated by two very famous names in its record: Nietzsche, the German philosopher who believed success could only come through cruelty and discipline, and Bergson, the French philosopher who taught that in the shining soul of man himself, reflecting the *élan vital* of the universe, lay the secret of human salvation. Both these great thinkers were very logical, quite impersonal, and utterly just in their findings. But Nietzsche was an apostle of intellectual darkness, and Bergson, of intellectual and spiritual light.

The philosophical mind seems to be habitual with the Libra FOURS. It is refreshing to find more cheerful souls such as P. G. Wodehouse, creator of 'Jeeves the butler', Art Buchwald, and Oscar Wilde on the roll. Others on this list include: Rimbaud, French symbolist poet; Franz Liszt, composer; C. P. Snow, novelist; Arthur Miller, playwright; Rita Hayworth, actress; David Ben-Gurion, Israeli leader; D. T. Suzuki, Zen Master; Samuel Taylor Coleridge, poet; and Nicholas Culpepper, English herbalist.

In everyday life, they are found to be delightful people, as long as the rest of us can live up to — or even approach — their rather high standards of excellence. They have a passion for order and perfection; they love symmetry and beauty, harmony and peace. The Tarot document endows them with 'quietness, rest, ease, and peace'. They dislike strife and quarrels, and they despise disorder and untidiness.

They have an unusually good sense of time; they avoid hurry and bustle. With their extraordinarily clear minds, they just can't see the sense of getting excited about the average subjects of human excitement. They automatically add, subtract and divide the values while other people are just beginning to wonder what it is all about.

But, in spite of its tendency toward philosophy and logic, the friendliness of the Jupiter frequency warms and lightens this personality with a sincere charm that makes a Libra FOUR not only a valuable and useful but also a highly desirable member of the human family.

'Rest From Strife'

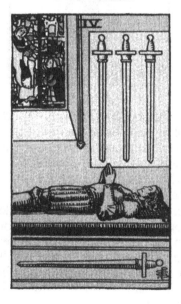

SCORPIO
(October 23 to November 22)

This Key does *not* represent a hanging! It expresses, forcibly, the power of individual thinking, as opposed to orthodox mass sentiment. The brightly-clad figure is reversed — upside down — but perfectly balanced, stable, and secure. Around his head glows the light of knowledge — illumination. The living tree from which he 'hangs' is a universal symbol for growth and development in life, YOUR life. The double implication of the Key for the three positive personalities born during the Scorpio Decanates is that individual freedom of thought and action will never result from violence or combat but from stability and vision, symbolized by his perfect balance, even while upside down, and the golden halo round the head of the Hanged Man.

FIVE of SCORPIO

October 23 to November 1   (0° to 9°59′ of ♏)

Potential: FIVE	Frequency: MARS
(Activity)	*(Activity)*

Basic Quality: WATER
(Flexibility)

Energy, friendliness, courage, and personal power are blended in this nature. The conflict lies between emotionalism and practical common sense.

On the positive side
This is a personality of great charm, highly emotional and affectionate, with a keen social sense and the gift of true friendliness. The Scorpio FIVES are generous, hospitable, tolerant, and sympathetic. They are eager to right wrongs and to help the unfortunate. They are tireless in work and in play; they have valour, initiative, and lively imaginations. They enjoy life to the full, and like to share their pleasures. They are persistently active, receptive to new ideas, open to suggestions. They have no sense of limitation in their own possibilities of achievement, and they are tremendous hard workers. They are apt to be popular and to have many friends.

On the negative side
They overdo everything — work, play, and physical pleasures. They are passionate rather than affectionate, dominant rather than helpful. They drive themselves and everybody else to exhaustion, and create around them an atmosphere of tension and discomfort. They become fanatical, especially along humanitarian lines, and they are apt to develop destructive ideas of progress. Negative, they lack discrimination and self-control, and are likely to waste their excellent energies in unworthy undertakings, or in excess of pleasure. They become quarrelsome, always taking the opposition, making enemies instead of friends. When completely negative, they can be treacherous and deceitful, ungrateful and untrustworthy.

Balance
Control of the emotions, temperance, and conservation of energy are the principal balancing factors for the Scorpio FIVES. They tend to go to extremes of joy or sorrow, kindness or cruelty, and only through self-control and the consistent exercise of discrimination can they keep in the middle of the road and steer a straight course through life. They need to keep a close watch over their destructive tendencies, and to develop, instead, their innate kindliness and sympathy. It is very hard for the Scorpio FIVES to be impersonal —

to separate their minds from their emotions and desires — and this very achievement of an impersonal viewpoint is their best way to balanced happiness and practical success.

Comment

The energy and force of the Mars frequency doubles the positive activity of the FIVE potential, producing in this case a decidedly strenuous personality. It has been found that the Scorpio FIVES can work more hours at a stretch, and get along with less sleep, than any other group in the pattern. Mars, in ancient mythology, was the god of war, and is popularly associated with the ideas of fighting, anger, and strife. A careful study of the symbols, however, as well as of the people born during cycles with Mars frequencies, has suggested that psychologically the force represented by Mars is a desire to change things for the better — even if considerable destructive damage has to be done as a part of the process. It is not surprising to find, among the well-known people born during this cycle, fanatical reformers, fighters, and untiring workers.

An interesting example is 'Big Stick' President Theodore Roosevelt; another is Dylan Thomas, fiery, self-destructive, genius. Jonas Salk is a Scorpio FIVE; so were Pablo Picasso, Chiang Kai-shek, the philosopher Erasmus; violinist Niccolo Paganini; and Admiral Richard E. Byrd, conqueror of that frozen wasteland, the Arctic. All are typical of the power and driving energy of this period.

It is, however, one of the few cycles whose title and picture constitute a warning. '*Loss in Pleasure*' is the name of the Tarot card, and the description reiterates the warning, with unusual emphasis on the negative side of the personality. The explanation of this seems to be that the Scorpio FIVES, with their tendency to overdo everything they undertake, are apt to undermine their own chances for success and happiness. The spilled cups in the picture are *not* a warning against wine; they are symbols of the disappointment which follows misdirected and uncontrolled energy, either in work or pleasure, in fighting evil or in emotional indulgence, in creating or destroying. It seems rather clear that the old-fashioned virtues of temperance and self-control are vital to the welfare of the Scorpio FIVE.

Personal study and analysis have revealed a strong emotional factor in these individuals, which sometimes makes for maladjustment to practical life. They feel so intensely that they forget to think; they desire so strongly that they neglect discrimination in following their impulses. Perhaps it is because they suffer so deeply when they find themselves out of balance that the Tarot document stresses their weakness rather than their strength, for there is no question about the force and power that is found in this personality. Their greatest gift is the one placed by an American psychologist at the top of the list of desirable human assets — the ability to be 'just folks'.

'Loss in Pleasure'

SIX of SCORPIO

November 2 to 12   (10° to 19°59′ of ♏)

Potential: SIX	Frequency: SUN
(Ambition)	*(Ambition)*

Basic Quality: WATER
(Flexibility)

Magnetic charm, showmanship, creative imagination, and staying power, are the principal factors in this nature. The conflict lies between the desire for personal achievement and an innate generosity and kindliness of heart.

On the positive side
This is a dominant personality, having a great power of attraction and a wide scope of potential achievement. Leadership comes naturally to the Scorpio SIXES; they take the centre of any stage, as by divine right, and occupy it successfully, with popularity and charm. They combine an indomitable will with a gentle manner; they conquer subtly, but inevitably; they possess the innate ability to get what they want. They are naturally generous, eager to share and to give; they are warmhearted and passionate in their affections. They are very hospitable, and they have a tremendous appetite for pleasure and enjoyment. They work and play with equal enthusiasm and ardour, and they attract admiration, friendship, and love, wherever they go. They carry the seed of success.

On the negative side
They are proud, intolerant, and self-assertive; they are cruel, inconsiderate and ruthless, having no regard for the feelings or sufferings of others. Their one desire is to succeed, to gain possession of what they want, or to get their own way by imposing their will on other people, and this desire is so strong that it outweighs everything else, especially kindness or justice. The negative Scorpio SIX is a sensualist, seeking personal gratification as the sole objective in life. This desire can be for power, for physical pleasures, or for wealth and material possessions, but whatever form it takes, it is a driving force of terrific energy, making the negative Scorpio SIX almost impossible to influence or change. They are invulnerable to suggestion or appeal, and they make formidable enemies.

Balance
The development and consistent practice of generosity and friendliness is the best balancing factor in the structure of the Scorpio SIXES. The quality of human affection and love is a dominant trait in their natures, and when they follow their natural impulses toward kindliness, their entire personality, with its potential force and power, is automatically equilibrated. Because of their ambition to be the

centre of attraction, the Scorpio SIXES are often in danger of overstepping the bounds of justice to others. But when balanced, they find that it adds considerably to their own attractive forces when they are kind, tolerant, and friendly. A balanced Scorpio SIX is gentle — with the gentleness that is born only of strength.

Comment
This cycle stands at the peak of the third wave of the solar year. Of all the peak periods — the SIXES — this one seems to contain the greatest creative power, and the most compelling charm. This can be attributed to the flexibility and gentleness of the Water quality, which here provides the necessary feminine, or receptive balance against the doubled masculine, or positive force of a Sun frequency and a SIX potential.

The famous names in this list tell their own story. We find here Martin Luther, whose drive undermined the influence of the Roman Catholic Church and resulted in his founding a new form of worship; Feodor Dostoevsky, writer of strangely impassioned, dark novels characterized by deep psychological insights and a morbid preoccupation with guilt, crime, and punishment; Mme. Marie Curie, physicist, chemist, and winner of two Nobel prizes, whose secret reserves of strength enabled her to persist in her search through many tons of ore to gather that mysterious radioactive substance known as uranium; Paracelsus, physician and alchemist, who travelled the world in search of the lost keys of healing; Leon Trotsky, Russian revolutionary leader; General George Patton, now legendary military leader during World War II; Billy Graham, evangelist; Albert Camus, Kurt Vonnegut, Jr., and Ivan Turgenev, novelists who strongly influenced the youths of their respective times; actresses Katharine Hepburn and Hedy Lamarr; Auguste Rodin, sculptor, who interpreted the physical as divine; Will Rogers and Jonathan Winters, both remarkable comedians.

The chief problem of the Scorpio SIX, in any department of life, seems to be the one of getting along with other people, particularly if the other people happen to be, for the moment, in the driver's seat. The average SIX does not take kindly to authority and discipline, even when it is obviously the only thing to do. And when this personality rebels, the vigour and enthusiasm displayed are quite as great as when these same forces are used to produce the notable successes of the cycle's roll of honour. In plain words, a negative Scorpio SIX, at any time, is a tough nut to crack.

But in all the pattern of the year, there is no more utterly charming personality than the balanced Scorpio SIX, functioning on the positive side of his or her nature. The possibilities for happiness and achievement, in this peak period of the third wave of the year's Solar energy, are so considerable that if it were possible to choose one's birthdate, this period would be a happy choice.

'Pleasure'

SEVEN of SCORPIO

November 13 to 22   (20° to 29°59′ of ♏)

Potential: SEVEN
(Versatility)

Frequency: VENUS
(Productivity)

Basic Quality: WATER
(Flexibility)

Instinctive personal charm, creative power, adaptability, and a strong will are the underlying factors of this personality. The conflict lies between the positive urge to create and a negative laziness — a desire for pleasure.

On the positive side
There is an element of greatness in this personality; its potentialities for achievement are widely varied, covering almost every field of creative endeavour. The positive Scorpio SEVENS learn very easily, absorbing new ideas with intensity and great speed. Their personal charm is so great as to give them the power to influence other people without apparent effort, and they attract affection and love wherever they go. They have keen sympathy for suffering, and an intuitive understanding of human desires and emotions. Their strength is subtle; their flexibility is resilience; their personal magnetism is a powerful attractive force. They have tremendous resistance and recuperative power. They are affectionate; they love, and desire to be loved, with passionate intensity.

On the negative side
They suffer from illusions; they believe in unrealities; they reject ideas of training and technique, learning and discipline. Their versatility becomes a fickle instability; they do not concentrate on any one thing long enough either to understand or to finish it. The negative Scorpio SEVENS are lazy, self-indulgent and deceitful; they depend on other people's efforts rather than their own; they evade responsibility and decisions; they lack initiative and courage; they fail to keep their bargains and to fulfill their promises. When very negative, they lose their sense of integrity and ethics, becoming selfish and irresponsible in their approach to life.

Balance
Creative activity, self-discipline, and the consistent holding of high ideals of behaviour and achievement, are the secrets of balance for the many-sided Scorpio SEVENS. Inactivity, inertia, and laziness of mind are the chief temptations to be resisted, and a self-imposed routine of effort toward some definite goal, great or small, mental or physical, is the method that will bring the best results. They need temperance rather than restriction, control of emotions and desires

rather than prohibition or asceticism. Balance, for the Scorpio SEVENS, is not easy, and it is vitally necessary for their welfare and success in life.

Comment

The word that is most often found linked with the number seven, in the symbolic writings, is *power*. In this cycle, the combination of the SEVEN potential with the Venus frequency (numbered seven) doubles the force of both factors — either one of which, alone, is enough to provide a personal quality of considerable potency to the individual concerned. All through the pattern, it has been found, the SEVEN potentials and the Venus frequencies call for self-discipline and self-control as their primary and most necessary achievement. The SEVEN is described in the Tarot document as '*a force transcending the material plane, like unto a crown, but requiring one capable of wearing it*' — which would seem to indicate, judging from analysis and study of these personalities in actual life, that this high-geared nature is rather like a pet tiger. Its owner has to tame it, or be destroyed by it. To be a successful Scorpio SEVEN is not a simple job; tigers are not easy animals to train, or to keep under control.

That it can be done, however, is shown by the famous names in the decanate's record. Their wide variety of interests is especially notable in view of the versatility characteristic of the cycle. Robert Louis Stevenson, a writer whose imagination has contributed to the enrichment of practically everyone's childhood; Claude Monet, the French impressionist painter of light and colour; Israel Regardie, occultist; André Gide, French writer and Nobel prize winner; Eugene Ormandy, American orchestra conductor; Oliver Goldsmith, wonderful English playwright of the eighteenth century; Indira Gandhi, Indian prime minister; Voltaire, eighteenth-century philosopher, historian, poet, dramatist, and sceptic; Erwin Rommel, German general, 'the Desert Fox'; and Sir William Herschel, English astronomer and discoverer of the planet Uranus.

The weakness of this nature, it has been found, is its quick receptivity and a lack of analytical and critical ability. The intuitive faculty of the Scorpio SEVENS is very active; they are given to having, and following, 'hunches'. But the difficulty, here, is that their personal desires are apt to be so strong that they automatically deflect the supposed 'hunch' in the direction most agreeable at the moment. It is usually found that failure, in the case of the SEVEN personalities, comes largely from their unwillingness to use their common sense, and to profit by painful experience. The quality of illusion in the nature of the Scorpio SEVENS causes them, rather often, to mistake the shadow for the substance in their choice of an objective.

But it will usually be found also that no matter what these individuals may do, or leave undone, they will be greatly beloved by a number of people, for the quality of affection in their natures is so strong that it acts as a magnet, receiving as well as giving love and friendship in no inconsiderable measure. And once a Scorpio SEVEN really makes up his or her mind as to an objective, and sticks

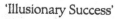

'Illusionary Success'

to it, there is practically nothing within the realm of reason — and sometimes even outside of it! — that is impossible of attainment.

SAGITTARIUS
(November 23 to December 21)

The name of this Key bears no relation to its modern meaning of prohibition — very much the reverse. It refers to an older meaning of the word: *tempering*, refining, improving, sharpening your personal factors for better use and performance. The picture clearly indicates that you have, at all times, a 'Guardian Angel' within you, ready with guidance from the four great forces — Fire (the sun) Water (flowing between the golden cups) Air (the growing flowers) and Earth, on which the Angel is careful to keep one foot, for equilibrium. The suggestion that all four of man's natural tools, or weapons, are in hand — and are essential — quite in tune with the dynamic individuals born during the Sagittarius Decanates. Also, it carries an instruction to use these powers constructively at all times, in harmony with the attitude and action of the winged figure — YOUR Angel.

EIGHT of SAGITTARIUS

November 23 to December 2	(0° to 9°59′ of ♐)

Potential: EIGHT	Frequency: MERCURY
(Sagacity)	*(Sagacity)*

Basic Quality: FIRE
(Dynamic Energy)

Keen intelligence, discrimination, quick reaction, and objectivity, are the principal factors in this nature. The conflict lies between impetuosity and logical foresight.

On the positive side
The Sagittarius EIGHTS are clearheaded, quick-witted, and practical. Their cleverness and dexterity are both mental and physical; they have good co-ordination of mind and body, and are naturally skillful with their hands as well as their brains. They are observant, perceptive, and analytical; they have initiative and determination; their approach to life is direct and uncompromising; they stick to facts and reject illusions. They are interpreters rather than creative workers, but they have a gift of expression, through speech or writing. They have executive ability; they are good detail workers; they are orderly and trustworthy. They are impersonally objective in their approach to problems, practical or personal. They have a dependable capacity for short-range foresight.

On the negative side
They are overdirect, impulsive, and short-sighted; they are extremely critical; they are hasty in decision and violent in action; they forget to use their own best quality of analytical discrimination. Their quick reaction becomes recklessness; their uncompromising approach develops into lack of consideration for the feelings and desires of others. Their cleverness reverts to cunning and trickery; their eloquence is used in evading responsibility; their skill and wit, in keeping out of trouble rather than for practical accomplishment. Negative, they are cold, unresponsive, very selfish, and intolerant.

Balance
Tolerance and patience are the best balance-producers for the

Sagittarius EIGHTS. Their natural approach to all problems is much more logical, and their reactions are swifter than the average, which means that they are apt to be harsh and impatient with people who are more emotional, and slower-thinking, than they are themselves. Also, these EIGHTS are apt to be impatient with time itself; their desire to push the clock ahead is one of their greatest factors of unbalance. To learn the art of waiting, and of understanding people with human as well as with intellectual sympathy, creates a balance for these high-strung personalities which makes possible both material success and personal happiness.

Comment
The double dose of sagacity — instinctive cleverness — in this personality creates a mental restlessness in the Sagittarius EIGHTS which is apt to be hard on other people as well as on themselves. They demand, of the world in general, logical and intelligent behaviour, which is a lot to ask of any world. And when the world — as it seems to them — lets them down, their bitter disappointment is apt to take disturbing forms. These individuals seem to have greater trouble even than most of us in managing successfully their human relationships. Just as they tend to demand too much of the world, so they demand an almost impossible perfection from their associates, particularly from the people they love.

They are not ambitious. The record of famous names in the cycle's roll of honour is one of the shortest in the year. The best known names in the brief list are Mark Twain, American humourist; Jonathan Swift, English satirist; Prime Minister Winston Churchill and American politician William F. Buckley, Jr.; English poet and artist, William Blake; beloved children's novelist Louisa May Alcott; comedians Harpo Marx and Woody Allen; and opera prima donna Maria Callas. Although it is difficult to generalize on a list such as this one, it is nevertheless a fact which stands out that the major quality shared by all these people is forthrightness of speech or manner and calling a 'spade a spade', in a witty fashion. This is especially true of Mark Twain and Jonathan Swift, for if any persons ever possessed the gift of using words and speech in aptly interpreting what they saw around them, these two are perfect examples.

Practically all the people born during these autumn cycles of similar potentials and frequencies, it has been found, have a tendency to exaggerate the expression of their basic factors. This is probably because of the lack of modification by contrasting or complementary factors, such as most of the cycles possess. With the Sagittarius EIGHTS, this tendency is especially noticetable, because the factor of directness is strengthened, not modified, by the dynamic energy of the quality of Fire.

'Swiftness'

Relaxation of tension, for them, is not easy to achieve, and high-strung nerves are often found to be the cause of many of their troubles and mistakes. The name of the Tarot card is '*Swiftness*'. The constant conflict in their natures between the impulsive desire to go ahead quickly, at all costs, and the restrictive discipline of their logical, analytical minds, contributes more fuel to the fires of tension, which often leads to an explosion of what seems to be bad temper, but is really the snapping of taut nerves — the only way of relieving the tie-up.

While they may not achieve fame in large numbers as a matter of record, these individuals are decidedly not nonentities. They are vital and forceful, with capacities for practical achievement above the average. But — possibly because of this — they need, more than the average, the balanced attitude toward life, which, for them, is one of tolerance and patience.

NINE of SAGITTARIUS

December 3 to 12   (10° to 19°59′ of ♐)

Potential: NINE	Frequency: MOON
(Dependability)	*(Adaptability)*

Basic Quality: FIRE
(Dynamic Energy)

Fortitude and personal charm, energy and intuition, with great dynamic force, are combined in this personality. The conflict lies between love of self-indulgent pleasure and desire for creative activity.

On the positive side
There is strength, with tremendous vitality and personal power, and great resistance, in the nature of the Sagittarius NINES. Their adaptability is resiliency — it is a positive adjustment, never yielding. They are very sensitive to impressions, and keenly intuitive, knowing what people want and how to give it to them. They are capable of wide and varied interests, and can succeed in almost anything they really want to do, by the use of concentrated and consistent effort. They are highly emotional, deeply affectionate, and very passionate. They have strong appetites, for work, play, or pleasure; they are hospitable and generous, friendly and companionable and usually popular with both sexes. Their dynamic, energetic approach to life is modified by their personal charm and human sympathy.

On the negative side
Their strength and resistance reverts to an unreasonable obstinacy; they go their own way regardless of evidence that it may be the wrong way. They follow their emotional impulses to the bitter end, taking unnecessary punishment, and dissipating their energies in worthless pursuits. They are self-indulgent, intemperate in pleasure,

undisciplined in behaviour. They are governed by their emotions and desires, and, when negative, are apt to lose their sense of direction, and swing from the extreme of optimism to the ultimate of gloom, uncontrolled and uncontrollable.

Balance

A sense of responsibility is the best possible balance wheel for the Sagittarius NINES. If they can direct their natural force and power into channels of controlled activity, consistently remembering their responsibility to themselves as individuals, to other people, and to life itself, they can achieve the balance needed to set free their own potential greatness. Emotional control is essential to their mental, physical, and spiritual welfare, as well as to their success in practical affairs, and to their personal happiness. Temperance, discrimination in pleasure, and disciplined, steady activity in work, enterprise, and in the simple matters of everyday living, are their keys to equilibrium, poise, and achievement.

Comment

Just as certain of the highly-charged personalities from other cycles can be likened to wild animals, difficult to tame, so the nature of the Sagittarius NINE is rather like a runaway steam engine. The rhythmic power of the Moon frequency — always associated with the symbol of Water — linked with its own potential number, and functioning through the dynamic quality of Fire, sets up a head of steam that is apt, unless well handled, to escape in wasted energy, and this is just what happens to the uncontrolled, undirected energies of the negative, or unbalanced Sagittarius NINES.

But, just as the same force, under mechanical control, has conquered continents, so can the tremendous vital factors of these individuals be turned to use in practical achievement. Their charm, their power over people, and their ability to sense 'what the public wants' are among their most valuable assets.

Walt Disney, who sensed that the world was hungry for fairy tales, worked hard all his life to feed that hunger. Disney is a particularly interesting example of the cycle's qualities, because the Moon is a symbol of *memory* and also of *fantasy*. Walt Disney gave the world Snow White, Pinocchio, and Ferdinand the Bull, as well as Mickey

Mouse. Other famous names in the cycle's record command a wide public, including James Thurber, the great humourist who acquired such a devoted following that even many years after his death, his name is still well known and loved; Emmet Kelly, the most famous clown of them all; Edward G. Robinson, actor; Joseph Conrad and Samuel Butler, novelists; Emily Dickinson, poetess; John Milton, whose inner vision was of such grandeur that his poetry has vastly enriched the English language.

The Tarot document promises to these dynamic individuals '*great success, but with strife and energy*', and credits them with '*tremendous and steady force that cannot be shaken*'. It also describes them, on the negative side, as '*intractable and obstinate*'.

Personal study and analysis have shown that these factors are very often found among the people born during this period. They can make friends and influence people so easily that they sometimes fall under the illusion that no further effort is necessary — forgetting that this famous gesture is only the beginning of true achievement. But when they accept the simple rules of human discipline, and keep

'Great Strength'

the engine running smoothly on the rails, with a firm hand on the throttle, their possibilities of success are unquestionably great. This is the only cycle of the year in which the creative intuition of the Moon frequency is activated and turned positive by the basic quality of Fire.

TEN of SAGITTARIUS

December 13 to 21   (20° to 29°59′ of ♐)

Potential: TEN   Frequency: SATURN
(Persistence)   *(Intensity)*

Basic Quality: FIRE
(Dynamic Energy)

Determination, dependability, constructive force, and a strong will, make up the structure of this character. The only conflict arises from the overpositive nature of all three factors in the structure.

On the positive side
This is a dominant, powerful, and very constructive personality. The Sagittarius TENS are geared for large undertakings, major enterprises, and heavy responsibilities. They combine energy with common sense, enthusiasm with logic, and initiative with patience. Their desires tend toward productive activity, along practical lines, and always they build for permanence, security, and safety. They prefer the conventional paths, the established forms, the orderly methods in life. They are trustworthy, intrinsically honest, ambitious for achievement rather than for fame. They have tremendous vitality, and possess the ability to influence, direct, and inspire the activities of others. They have natural administrative ability, broad vision, and high ideals. They are good disciplinarians, loyal friends, and they have a strong sense of ethical, family, and community responsibility.

On the negative side
They are intolerant, cruel, and overbearing, impatient with weakness, unsympathetic with suffering; instead of accepting responsibility, they pile it up on other people, with lack of consideration and an overemphasis on discipline. When negative, they take the opposition at all times; they reject new ideas, suggestions, and criticisms; they

are unadaptable and obstinate, dogmatic and dictatorial. They desire always to hold a dominant position, either in practical or personal affairs, or in family life, and they are apt to be ruthless in their methods of gaining this desire. They are unyielding in the matter of opinion; they are convinced of their own integrity, and they do not hesitate to impose their will on others.

Balance
The development of the quality of human sympathy is the secret of balance for these powerful personalities. True strength is always kind; the extraordinary power of this personality can only be put to its fullest and best use when severity is tempered by mercy, and discipline is softened by gentleness and tolerance. Activity, and consistent striving toward a constructive goal, are necessary to keep the overpositive energies from turning in upon themselves in bitterness and anger. Adaptability, receptivity, and above all, a sense of humour, will equilibrate the Sagittarius TENS, and thus increase their happiness as well as their efficiency.

Comment
With this cycle, the personality factors once again take on a greater variety of modification than has been the case with the preceding seven, in which the frequency and the potential were similar in psychological quality. But there is such a strong similarity between the persistent determination of the TEN potential and the integrative intensity of the Saturn frequency that even here there seems to be a particularly one-pointed, single-minded force at work in the structure of the personality. This force is stimulated rather than modified by the dynamic energy of the basic quality of Fire.

The combination of all these forceful factors results in a notably strong personality. In the ancient science called 'alchemy' the Saturn force is said to be of the nature of *salt*. And it would appear, from the sturdy qualities belonging to the positive side of the Sagittarius TEN, that they could be described as 'the salt of the earth'. But it must also be remembered that an overdose of salt is a strenuous thing to cope with — and so is the negative side of this nature.

Only a modest number of famous names appear in the cycle's record, but there are notable names among these few. It is believed that Nostradamus, the greatest astrological prophet of history, was born during this period — he never revealed the secret of his system. The modern philosopher George Santayana was born on December 16th, and so were Beethoven, Jane Austen, Noel Coward, and anthropologist Margaret Mead.

Other distinguished Sagittarius TENS include Gustav Flaubert, French author; Jean Paul Getty, one of the world's richest men; Saki, the British writer of those strange, funny short stories; Paul Klee, the artist; Racine, classic French dramatist; Jean Genêt, playwright of a more 'modern' temperament; Disraeli, the British statesman; and David Susskind, American TV moderator and film producer.

There is something very solid about the people born during this period. The picture shows a man carrying a very heavy burden, and evidently quite capable of doing it. While the name of the card is '*Oppression*' — obviously referring to the negative side of the character — the description ends up on the positive side by crediting the Sagittarius TENS with '*generosity, disinterestedness, and self-sacrifice*'. Their chief difficulty, it seems, is the tendency so often found with

'Oppression'

the Saturn frequencies, to take everything too seriously. The kind word, the light touch, and friendly laughter, are the best magic, at any time, for the Saturn individual to use. These turn the 'salt' of the Saturn force into a pleasant flavour, never bitter on the tongue, but savoury and good with everything it touches.

CAPRICORN
(December 22 to January 19)

The frightening aspect of this Key is one of the many touches of humour in the Tarot. The grotesque figure with horns, batwings, and cloven hooves, looks alarming enough until you notice, first, that the man and woman seem quite unperturbed, and second, that the chains, apparently binding them to the black stone of the Devil's footstool, are so loose that they can easily be lifted over the head. The word is clear: 'Evil is in the eye of the beholder'. The Devil is merely an adversary, strengthening the muscles of the mind. He can best be conquered by the realization that every apparent evil is actually the *negative side* of a corresponding good. The human figures, representing YOU, have only to lift their chains to be free from the bondage of erroneous ideas and interpretations leading, so often, to mistaken actions. The Key provides a logical background for the Capricorn Decanates — strong, stable, and positive, each in its own way.

TWO of CAPRICORN

December 22 to 30   (0° to 9°59′ of ♑)

Potential: TWO   Frequency: JUPITER
(Initiative)   *(Stability)*

Basic Quality: EARTH
(Practical Sense)

Diplomacy, adaptability, poise, and resourcefulness are the
main factors of this character. The conflict lies between the
desire for practical achievement and a restless instability of
purpose.

On the positive side
Many of the most agreeable of the human qualities are found in this
personality. The Capricorn TWOS are gentle, instinctively courteous,
and very hospitable. They have an intuitive understanding of other
people's emotions, and their sympathy is spiced with humour. They
have a gift for happiness and the enjoyment of life; they appreciate
the simple, basic, physical pleasures. They have a strong sense of
fair play in human relationships, in business, and in practical matters.
They are merciful, but just; they are generous, but wise in their giving.
They are affectionate, and usually very popular, having many
acquaintances and friends. They can adapt themselves to different
levels of living with unconscious ease. They are democratic and
tolerant in their approach to life, and their practical sense is strong
and active.

On the negative side
They exhibit indecision and uncertainty of purpose. They swing from
one side of a question to the other so readily that they do not know
their own minds. Their natural tact and diplomacy weakens to a
willingness to agree with anyone or anything — the diplomat
becomes a yes-man. Their adaptability, when negative, is apt to bring
in a lack of judgment; they yield to circumstances without analyzing
the conditions of calculating the results. They are apt to experience
sudden impulses toward self-indulgence, in which they lose their
poise completely and go to the opposite extreme of nervous
instability. When negative, they give the impression of weakness and

timidity, and they suffer from fear of the future.

Balance

Persistent honesty and integrity, with the determination to know exactly where they are going, and to pursue a definite objective, is the key to balance for the Capricorn TWOS. Their natural poise is easily retained as long as they are not swayed back and forth by indecision, and their naturally good judgment will always function if they refuse to be unduly influenced by other people or by mass opinion. The temptation of yielding to a desire for 'peace at any price' has to be overcome, and the Capricorn TWOS need to remember to be fair to themselves as well as kind to others. Impulsive action is one of their worst pitfalls — difficult though it is for them to make up their minds, they have to learn to look before they leap.

Comment

This is the cycle in which is found the birthday of the Man who has been called the Prince of Peace. Its symbols are fully in harmony with the ideals of Christmas — peace on earth, good will toward men, kindness and generosity, mercy rather than severity. It has been found that there is a sweetness and gentleness in the nature of the Capricorn TWOS — positive or negative, well or less well balanced — that is very suggestive of the principle known as the Golden Rule.

In balance, the Capricorn TWOS are exceedingly fine characters. There is no real conflict between the four-square stability of the Jupiter frequency, the integrated power of the Earth quality, and the initiative and resourcefulness of the TWO potential. The principal difficulty encountered by these individuals is that they are in a minority, desiring peace and good will in a world rather thickly populated with people whose demands are very different. Study and personal analysis have shown that when a Capricorn TWO is ultranegative, and weak, it is usually because of over-sensitiveness to the normal cruelties of life. There is no other period in the year in which there is less suggestion of hatred, anger, or any destructive emotions than in this one. And, while it makes them very delightful and charming people, this puts the Capricorn TWOS at something of a disadvantage in a rough-and-tumble world.

The famous names in the cycle's birthday record show the widely varied possibilities in its adaptable, poised personalities. Rudyard Kipling, poet, novelist, and Nobel prize winner; Robert Ripley of 'Believe It or Not' fame; timeless stars Marlene Dietrich and Ava Gardner; Sir Isaac Newton, genius; the astronomer Kepler; Louis Pasteur, French chemist and biologist; Henri Matisse, French painter and sculptor; Pablo Casals, cellist; Howard Hughes was also born during this decanate; and so was Mao Tse-tung, chairman of Communist China. Helena Rubinstein, cosmetics queen who created a financial empire, is another Capricorn TWO.

It has been found that the Capricorn TWOS are usually very charming, attractive to the opposite sex, popular and well liked in both business and social life. In their closer personal relationships they are apt to be fickle, but when opposed, they can be astonishingly obstinate. Under their gentleness and charm there is an integrated strength of character which, when positively used, and not pushed or overstrained, is a dependable producer of success and happiness. As the Tarot document puts it, these individuals are *'fortunate through prudence of management'*.

'Harmonious Change'

THREE of CAPRICORN

December 31 to January 9   (10° to 19°59′ of ♑)

Potential: THREE   Frequency: MARS
(Determination)   *(Activity)*

Basic Quality: EARTH
(Practical Sense)

Constructive energy, creative ability, courage, and dependability, are the inherent characteristics of this nature. The conflict is a very normal one — it lies between emotional desire and practical common sense.

On the positive side

The creative fire in this personality is a controlled, constructive force, giving to the Capricorn THREES the ability to accomplish anything — within reason — that they undertake. They have the gift of accepting limitations, but overcoming them at the same time. They can keep their equilibrium in the midst of intense activity, and they are especially dependable in emergencies. They combine initiative with the desire to integrate and finish whatever they start; they are good workers, energetic and enthusiastic. They are naturally self-disciplined — their emotional force, while very powerful, is kept in hand by common sense and a strong will. In human relationships they are passionate, affectionate, and deeply sympathetic. They have an instinctive understanding of people and human conditions, and are always eager to improve conditions around them.

On the negative side

They are overpositive, domineering, and rebellious. They give full vent to such emotions as anger and jealousy, greed and hatred. They are so determined on their own course that they destroy anything which stands in their way, without regard for consequences or wreckage. Their creative fire turns thoroughly destructive. Their human sympathy becomes a dark pessimism that sees no good in anything; they turn in upon themselves, tending to develop solitary, exclusive habits that lead to loneliness. They indulge in a sense of superiority, making enemies instead of friends. When negative, the Capricorn THREES are unhappy people, and, because of their strong personal forces, they can cause great misery to those around them.

Balance

Recognition of their own strength, and the determination to use it constructively at all times, is the first step toward balance for the Capricorn THREES. Avoidance of destructive thoughts and actions, and the development of the gentler qualities of life, are vitally necessary. Tolerance and patience — both of which are apt to be recessive qualities in their natures — should be practiced and encouraged. Most of all, relaxation is required for their balanced well-being: the letting-down of tension, taking time off for laughter and pleasure. A variety of interests, hobbies, and friendships, provides excellent equilibration for these positive, energetic people, whose tendency always is to be too definitely pointed in one direction to the exclusion of all others.

Comment

The structure of this personality is rather like a highly geared engine, requiring a skillful hand at the controls. With so much creative power in the pattern of the cycle, it is surprising to find comparatively few names in the record of its famous birthdays, but personal study of many individuals born during the cycle provided several reasons for this phenomenon. The personality is so powerful that it is decidedly a difficult one to manage, and its basic factors do not include any suggestion of ambition. Also, the negative tendencies toward quarreling, anger, and jealousy are not conducive to popular success, though they need not inhibit great constructive achievement.

Three powerful personalities with birthdays in this period who have attained both fame and achievement are Rudolf Bing, former Metropolitan Opera Company Manager; J. Edgar Hoover, founder of the F.B.I.; and Konrad Adenauer, German statesman. Quite a few artists and writers are included: Balanchine, J. D. Salinger, E. M. Forster, Carl Sandburg, Alan Watts, and Simone de Beauvoir — idealists in form and structure. Two humourists, Max Eastman and Victor Borge, are in the THREE cycle as well.

The Capricorn THREES have the primitive streak that is found with all Mars frequencies, and which produces a strength and driving force that is different from any other. These individuals dislike inactivity or lethargy, with the result that they are apt to neglect the matter of rest and relaxation, and to wind themselves up to such a pitch that the engine stalls. The best possible object lesson for a Capricorn THREE is to watch the incoming tide on a beach, and note that each wave backs off before making its next attempt to push further up on the shore.

It has been found that the Capricorn THREES, as a rule, need plenty of physical exercise, out of doors and close to nature. If they don't get it, they store up too much energy, and become quarrelsome. They are pre-eminently practical, and they work best with a definite, objective goal in view. In spite of the fact that the Tarot picture shows an artist at work, the document credits the personality with 'gain in commercial transactions, rank, increase of substance, influence, cleverness in business'. And it adds, with its usual blunt frankness, on the negative side, that they are 'selfish, narrow and prejudiced, given to seeking impossibilities'.

With a nature so highly charged on the positive, or masculine side,

'Material Works'

it seems that the best way of balance is to develop and encourage the receptive, feminine qualities which are a part of the creative ability that is so definite a factor of this personality. And, judging from the Tarot's promises, above, it would seem to be well worth the effort.

FOUR of CAPRICORN

January 10 to 19   (20° to 29°59' of ♑)

Potential: FOUR	Frequency: SUN
(Stability)	*(Ambition)*

Basic Quality: EARTH
(Practical Sense)

Logic, integrity, tenacity, and idealism, are the strongest factors in this nature. The conflict takes place between idealism — the desire for perfection — and common sense — the desire for practical and immediate success.

On the positive side

This is a very strong character. Capricorn FOURS combine the practical ability to take advantage of opportunities with a farsighted vision and logical caution. They are orderly, constructive, and productive. They are objective thinkers, steady workers, and their ambition is always directed toward a concrete tangible goal. They are trustworthy and exceedingly honest, with a passion for fair dealing in all human relationships. They have a strong sense of personal dignity, good executive ability, and a determination to finish anything they start. They have a natural sense of practical values; they are money-makers. In their personal relationships they are quietly friendly, patient, and very loyal.

On the negative side

They are overbearing and dominating. Their desire for perfection and justice turns wrong side out into severity and even cruelty. They think logically, but within a narrow, circumscribed range beyond which they will not venture. Their dignity expands to pride and oversensitiveness, and their lack of flexibility develops into obstinacy and intolerance. In their desire to complete the job at hand, they lose their perspective, and become entangled in the immediate picture.

Their gift for money-making, when negative, turns to greed and fear of loss, so that they grasp at the nearest profit and lose the ultimate fortune. When negative, the Capricorn FOURS are concerned with practical affairs to the exclusion of everything else.

Balance

These individuals possess two natural equilibrators — their sense of logic and their innate stability. If they develop their gifts for analyzing and measuring every situation as it arises, and exercise at all times their discrimination, they can achieve an excellent balance, and thus allow the happiness of the Sun frequency — which is apt to be inhibited by the practical qualities of Earth and the limitation of the FOUR potential — to shine through and create a genuine enjoyment of life. Tolerance and mercy, which are recessive qualities in this nature, should be assiduously cultivated if the balance is to be maintained, and the positive side of the personality kept uppermost.

Comment

In a practical world, it would seem that the Capricorn FOURS are the real salt of the earth. They are money-makers, but they are honest; they are ambitious, but their ambitions are practical and far-reaching, usually including the welfare of others as well as their own. Only a completely negative individual born during this cycle is ever found to be entirely selfish. There is a strain of generosity in every Sun frequency, and there is also a tendency toward idealism. In the case of the Capricorn FOURS, however, it has been found that these agreeable frequency factors, being in the minority, sometimes require a little special encouragement to show themselves. The strength of the personality is unquestionable — but the sweetness, as in the case of the lion in the fable, frequently has to be added in the form of honey.

A very distinguished company answers the roll call of the Capricorn FOURS. Alexander Hamilton, Benjamin Franklin, Albert Schweitzer, Molière, William James, Edgar Allan Poe, Anton Chekhov, A. A. Milne, author of children's books, Paul Cézanne, Danny Kaye, Galina Ulanova, Russian dancer, as well as rock star Janis Joplin, Al Capone, Robert E. Lee, and the everpopular poetic pugilist Muhammad Ali are all among their number.

This cycle is fairly close to the peak of famous births, which comes in February. Possibly because of the power innate in the personality of the Capricorn FOURS, it contains the second highest average of famous names in the mid-winter period. The ambition of the Sun frequency, helped along by the practical Earth quality, and buttressed by the stability and honesty of the FOUR potential, provides an almost perfect structure for success. This cycle, with its fine record of achievement, bears out rather clearly the truth of the old saying that honesty is the best policy.

But when it comes to the matter of personal happiness, study and analysis have shown that the Capricorn FOURS demand so much of life that they are apt to meet with frequent disappointment. The desire of the FOUR potential is for order, balance, security and justice; that of the Sun frequency is for beauty and perfection, while the Earth quality demands tangible results and an integrated structure, or it is not satisfied. All of which, in an imperfect world, might be described as rather a large order!

It may be that this very factor of idealism is the secret of the greatness of these personalities — they 'hitch their wagon to a star'; they will

'Earthly Power'

not take illusion for reality; they refuse to accept substitutes. They demand from life all that they are willing to put into it, and that is saying a good deal.

The Tarot document promises them 'success, rank, dominion, earthly power', and it has been found that they can achieve — when balanced — considerable happiness and satisfaction as well as material objectives in life.

AQUARIUS
(January 20 to February 18)

The personal implication of this Key is simple and direct; it can be summed up in one word — *awareness*. The nude figure is so fully aware of herself as a person that she needs no dress or ornament. At the same time she is aware that the pool must be filled, the ground needs water for grass and flowers, and that the stars are in the sky as part of the natural order of life. The little bird, singing on the bush, is an ibis — the bird of the Greek god of wisdom, Hermes, known to us as Mercury. Note that Mercury is the Frequency of the central, or peak Decanate of Aquarius, which is the birth-time of more *famous* people than any other in the year. Your birthday gift from the Star (traditionally the 'water-bearer') is more than self-discovery. It is *awareness* of yourself as a part of the evolutionary pattern of life.

FIVE of AQUARIUS

January 20 to 29   (0° to 9°59′ of ♒)

Potential: FIVE	Frequency: VENUS
(Activity)	*(Productivity)*

Basic Quality: AIR
(Mentality)

Creative energy, quick reactions, versatility, and instinctive charm are blended in this personality. The conflict takes place between the desire for power and achievement and the desire for personal pleasure.

On the positive side

There is a creative artist in every FIVE of Aquarius. They are emotional, sensitive, and imaginative; they are hard workers, discriminating thinkers, and constructive in their desires. They have strong personal magnetism, especially for the opposite sex, and they have the ability to influence, inspire, and direct the activities of others. They are passionate in their loyalties, and are always ready to fight for their convictions. They have tremendous energy, quick minds, and a strong sense of beauty. They are very versatile, usually capable of succeeding in a number of different directions. They are among the rare people who can do several things at a time and do them all well. They are very critical of their own efforts and those of others; they are hard to satisfy; they have a driving desire to change things for the better.

On the negative side

They are temperamental, high-strung, and easily irritated. They are over-sensitive to criticism, and constantly imagine themselves to be slighted, misunderstood, and even persecuted. They are fickle in their affections, and are apt to be cruel and inconsiderate in personal relationships. They are quarrelsome, suspicious, and unreliable. In their driving desire for change or improvement they become thoughtlessly destructive, only intent on breaking down existing conditions without any idea of reconstruction. When negative, they are apt to develop radical tendencies, and to be receptive to subversive and dangerous ideas.

Balance

The selection of a congenial channel — or channels — for the creative energies is the secret of balance for the Aquarius FIVES. When their vitality has not a sufficient or a satisfactory outlet, it piles up like an underground fire, and sooner or later explodes, or breaks out in some destructive activity — or in self-indulgence, breaking down health and character. Disciplined activity, plus control of the emotions, especially of anger, keeps these forceful individuals in equilibrium, and sets free their best creative qualities. The objective development of their mental capacities is also a balancer; they need to cultivate the art of thinking.

Comment
It seems that a birthdate in this cycle carries with it a considerable responsibility. Its famous names are of outstanding greatness; and personal study of many of its less famous representatives has suggested that its subtly dynamic forces are not easy to control and to equilibrate in everyday life. The curious fact that the Tarot document names the card '*Defeat*', in the face of its unquestionably powerful factors, may indicate that unless the individual conquers the negative side of his nature, defeat is apt to follow. The picture is clearly that of a fighter who has conquered his enemies, but who seems to feel a lack of confidence in his victory. To be a successful FIVE of Aquarius is not, it would appear, an easy job. But that it can be done is proved by the record of the people who have done it.

The legendary composer, Mozart, as well as two of the greatest contemporary musicians, Yehudi Menuhin and Artur Rubinstein are Aquarius FIVES. Also two great poets, of older fame, Robert Burns and Lord Byron. Writers Lewis Carroll, Somerset Maugham, August Strindberg, Stendhal, Edith Wharton, Virginia Woolf, and Jules Feiffer, satirist, grace the list. Two artists, Jackson Pollock and Édouard Manet; one cinematographer, the great Sergei Eisenstein; an English philosopher, Francis Bacon; and the sublime mystic Swedenborg add to this very distinguished roll of honour. The American president McKinley was born on January 29th.

The factors in the personality of the Aquarius FIVE are especially interesting because they represent a pair of polar opposites — the positive, masculine FIVE potential and the negative, feminine Venus frequency. When the personality is balanced, these factors are complementary, and provide an excellent combination of a creative, happy life. Out of balance, however, they are in constant opposition, and then the personality tends to extremes, veering from positive to negative and back again with disconcerting violence. Self-control is a primary requirement for every FIVE potential, and concentration

'Defeat'

is apt to be a recessive trait in any Venus frequency. So, in this period, which combines the FIVE with the Venus force, both these faculties call for conscious development, both for the direction of the fiery energies of the FIVE potential in constructive channels, and to overcome the tendency toward a scattering of energy, arising from the Venus frequency.

The mental equipment of the Aquarius FIVES is naturally good, and when they exert their keen wits in the direction and control of their powerful and varied personal forces, they can get from life not only success, but a rich, all-round fulfillment of their potentialities. Any cycle, of course, can produce a genius. But the chances are just a bit better than average in the case of the FIVE of Aquarius.

SIX of AQUARIUS

January 30 to February 8   (10° to 19°59′ of ♒)

Potential: SIX	Frequency: MERCURY
(Ambition)	*(Sagacity)*

Basic Quality: AIR
(Mentality)

Self-confidence, magnetic charm, intelligence, and the ability for leadership, are harmoniously combined in this picture. The only indicated conflict takes place between honesty and dishonesty. This cycle is the high point of the year's peak of famous births.

On the positive side

A sense of power, a clear, quick mind, and an unshakable confidence in their own ability, give to the Aquarius SIXES a quality of almost invulnerable strength. They have great personal charm, instinctive self-control, poise and dignity. They are highly-charged, energetic, tireless workers, never losing sight of their goal. They possess the unusual combination of an active, vivid imagination and a logical mentality, which suggests that the balance between the 'conscious' and the 'unconscious' minds, with them, is unusually even. They are idealists and individualists; they have a strong sense of showmanship. They have the gift of speech; they know the magic of words, spoken or written. They have the innate ability to attract to themselves anything — within reason — that they want.

On the negative side

A ruthless, dominating desire for mastery, and a complete lack of consideration for other people's feelings, ideas, or needs, is the wrong-side-out expression of this personality. Negative, the Aquarius SIXES are cold, impersonal, and cruel. They are egotistical, intolerant, and selfish. They are unduly sensitive to criticism, unforgiving and revengeful. They are mischievous, using their quick minds and active imaginations in destructive plots and plans. Wrong-side-out, they are apt to be thoroughly unscrupulous.

Balance

A sense of responsibility and fair play is one of the best balancing factors for this personality. Egotism should be tempered by generosity, and pride by tolerance. Personal poise and dignity should be cultivated, and always practiced, as without them the Aquarius SIXES lose that subtle quality of leadership that is one of their finest assets. Sincerity, kindness, and consideration for other people should be conscientiously developed, as these individuals are apt to be absorbed in their own personal ambitions to the exclusion of everything and everybody else.

Comment
With such a galaxy of famous names to the credit of this cycle, it would seem that the dice are loaded, from birth, in favour of the Aquarius SIXES. But the picture on the card, and its name, dispel at once any such illusion. The boatman is energetically poling his own boat toward the shore of the promised land, and in the boat, where he can keep an eye on them, are his wife, his child, and the six swords, presumably the fruits of battle.

'*Earned Success*' surely indicates that work, and hard work, produce the results promised to the individuals born during the year's peak of famous nativities. And the known facts bear out this indication. Not one of the notables in the imposing record of current achievement had fame fall into his lap like a ripe plum. The facts show that they all worked for it. The Tarot document pormises them '*success after anxiety and trouble*'.

No musician ever reached the top without work. Violinists Fritz Kreisler and Jascha Heifetz, as well as the great opera star Renata Tebaldi, are all Aquarius SIXES. Felix Mendelssohn the felicitous composer; Charles Dickens, the legendary novelist; John Ruskin, brilliant English essayist and Victorian social critic; James Joyce, Irish novelist and poet; Franz Schubert, Austrian composer; Norman Rockwell, American artist; J. K. Huysmans, fantastic French novelist; Sir Thomas More, writer, and Martin Buber, Jewish philosopher, are among the stars that shine on this list. Politicians past and present swell the record: Aaron Burr, Horace Greeley, American presidents William Harrison, Franklin D. Roosevelt and Ronald Reagan. Then there are B. V. Spassky, Russian chessmaster; Francois Truffaut, French film director; writers John Ford, Gertrude Stein, Norman Mailer, Jules Verne, and Alfred Adler. Two great astrologers, Evangeline Adams and C. E. O. Carter, join the list which includes more of the people who are listed in biographical dictionaries because more are born at this time of the year than at any other. In this particular research, among five hundred names of famous people, familiarly known, twenty per cent turned out to be SIXES, and of these, nearly one-third are found in the Aquarius SIX cycle.

'Earned Success'

Why should this be? Are they just lucky, or is there an explanation in the psychological structure for this apparently uncanny ability to succeed? Personal study of a considerable number of these individuals in private life, as well as close analysis of those in public life, has suggested that the explanation is to be found in the indications of the Tarot symbols of the cycle.

The success of the Aquarius SIXES can be attributed to the fact that success. They are self-confident, and therefore always optimistic. They are ambitious, and recognize no limitations. They are able to think — to analyze, to define, to differentiate between one course of action and another. They are willing to work for what they want, and, perhaps most important of all, they usually *know what they want*, which is a much rarer phenomenon than anyone but an investigator of human problems ever knows or realizes.

These are the people who succeed; the record shows it. But isn't it possible that the analysis of the Aquarius SIX can provide for all of us, no matter when we are born, a suggestive additional formula for success?

SEVEN of AQUARIUS

February 9 to 18   (20° to 29°59′ of ♒)

Potential: SEVEN   Frequency: MOON
(Versatility)   *(Adaptability)*

Basic Quality: AIR
(Mentality)

Facile cleverness, intuitive human understanding, independence, and creative imagination, are the principal factors in this nature. The conflict lies between desire for dominance and desire for pleasure.

On the positive side

This is a well-equipped personality of agreeable charm, many-sided capacity, and quick, intuitive intelligence. The Aquarius SEVENS have a keen, instinctive understanding of human desires; they are responsive and sympathetic, but also inspiring and dominating in their relationships with people — either personal or public. They have creative energy, vivid imagination, and indomitable optimism. They have no sense of limitation; their faith in humanity and in themselves is like a strong, invulnerable force. They are idealists, humanitarians, and dreamers, but with the will to work toward making their dreams come true. They are emotional and sensitive, desiring happiness and pleasure for themselves, and for others, far more than fame or wealth. They are generous, hospitable, and extremely adaptable.

On the negative side

They are insincere, undependable, and fickle, deceiving themselves as well as other people. They believe in illusions and unrealities, taking a superficial viewpoint toward life. They are impractical, impulsive, and changeable, lacking in responsibility and incapable of sustained or concentrated effort. When negative, they are self-indulgent in physical pleasures, lacking in self-control and personal dignity, and generally untrustworthy. Their intuitive cleverness reverts to cunning, and their charm is used as a weapon to impose their will on others, and for selfish gain.

Balance

Discrimination and concentration are the two most useful balancing factors in the structure of the Aquarius SEVENS — the right choice of an objective, and the determination to stick to one thing until it is finished. Balance, in this case, can best be attained through positive mental effort, by keeping the imagination within bounds, and by training the intuition against 'hunches' that are illusive and unreal. Self-discipline, especially in matters of desire and emotion, with orderly activity and accuracy of effort, are necessary elements of equilibrium — along with a persistently high standard of ethics and behaviour.

Comment

This cycle is one of the most complex in the pattern — and to appreciate this it is only necessary to remember how many different biographers have tried to interpret its most famous American, Abraham Lincoln, and that his personality, the man himself, still remains a mystery. There is something elusive about the Aquarius SEVENS: now you have them, now you don't. Just as you are beginning to understand them they seem to turn into somebody else, under your very eyes. The combination of symbols in the cycle is such as to create a baffling picture: the changeability of the Moon frequency, plus the unstable versatility of the SEVEN potential, functioning through the cool, impersonal freedom of the Air quality, add up to nothing much more than a question mark. Even the writer of the Tarot document was evidently puzzled by this personality, as the description is somewhat contradictory, and rather negative. But the positive side of the picture suggests a personality of rare charm, having just such possibilities of greatness as appeared in the nature of Abraham Lincoln.

Other great names are in the record — not in such numbers as in the preceding cycle, there being no factor of ambition in the SEVEN. A great scientist heads the list, Thomas A. Edison. Then there is Charles Darwin, who helped change the tempo of his times through his thoughts; Alfred North Whitehead, famous writer on religion; Grant Wood, the artist who painted the spirit of an American tradition, 'American Gothic'; John Barrymore, Andrés Segovia, classical guitarist; Charles Lamb, English essayist and critic; and

Galileo, the scientist who had the vision but not quite the strength to battle the ignorance of his time. And, on the less serious side, we find also among the cycle's famous names: Jimmy Durante, Jack Benny, Edgar Bergen, and the great character actor, portrayer of Mark Twain and Abraham Lincoln, Hal Holbrook. The cycle's latest candidate for the Hall of Fame may be Yoko Ono, pop artist.

As with all SEVEN potentials, versatility is at once the strength and the weakness of this personality. The combination of versatility with the receptive adaptability of the Moon frequency may be one of the reasons for the discouraging phrases found in the Tarot description — such as '*partial success. Inclination to lose when on the point of gaining, through not continuing the effort*'. The problem of balance, however, seems to boil down to the very simple process of objective concentration: of sticking to a job, or an ideal, once it is undertaken, and first, of course, of selecting the job or the ideal with intelligence and discrimination. The name of this cycle is '*Unstable Effort*', suggesting energy and strength as well as instability. It seems obvious that considerable success and happiness can be attained by the

'Unstable Effort'

Aquarius SEVEN who will take the trouble to concentrate, direct, and discipline the widely varied forces — and charm — of his or her personality.

PISCES
(February 19 to March 20)

This Key is a picture of change, growth, evolution, and development — the essential factors in every form of life on earth. Evolution, from the primeval crustacean crawling out of the water on to land, all the way to the human individual, whose face is profiled in the Moon — and what a Moon! Both new and full, golden like the Sun, exuding rays of energy, positive and negative (long and short) as well as dripping with the moisture needed by a fruitful earth. The wolf and dog, baying at the moon, represent nature both untamed and tamed, developed by human intelligence. That path between the two Towers, rising and falling, is the Tarot symbol of the ever-changing way that every one of us must follow, to gain the mountain peak of fulfillment and achievement — YOUR way, YOUR goal in life since the moment you were born.

EIGHT of PISCES

February 19 to 28   (0° to 9°59′ of ✕)

Potential: EIGHT   Frequency: SATURN
(Sagacity)   *(Intensity)*

Basic Quality: WATER
(Flexibility)

Constructive intelligence, compassion, intensity, and practical executive ability, are the outstanding factors in this nature. The conflict lies between logical common sense and personal sympathy.

On the positive side

This is a personality of quiet, persistent strength, dependable, resourceful, and trustworthy, but very sensitive. The Pisces EIGHTS are idealists, but they are practical in their approach to life, and always constructive in their desires. They are objective, logical, analytical, and clear-sighted, very fair and just in all human relationships, business or personal. They are mentally intuitive; they have a keen sense of values, in small things and great. They are accurate, meticulous workers, with a gift for detail, and a dominant sense of order and responsibility. They have an instinctive understanding of sorrow, and a strong desire to alleviate suffering and to improve conditions. They are loyal, patriotic, and conservative; but they are also clever and imaginative, having a sense of beauty and rhythm, creative power, and artistic sensibility.

On the negative side

They are intolerant and narrow-minded, self-righteous and unfriendly. They are ultracritical of other people's ideas, behaviour, and actions; they take life much too seriously, and tend toward pessimism. They have a shortened vision; the immediate future blinds them to the ultimate results; they get caught in the web of details; they expend too much energy in small things, thus inhibiting their natural intelligence and executive capacities. When negative, their human sympathy turns destructive, taking the form of cruelty and bitterness toward people who do not conform to their rigid standards, and of intense skepticism toward new ideas.

Balance

As with all the Saturn frequencies, the best balancing factor for the Pisces EIGHTS is a sense of humour. Laughter, a willingness to see both sides of a human problem or viewpoint, along with a friendly tolerance of other people's peculiarities, make an excellent equilibrating combination for these serious-minded individuals. They need to lighten even their sympathy and compassion with humour — or it is apt to do more harm than good — and in all personal matters, laughter and the lighter touch will be found most efficacious in adjusting human relationships, as well as in bringing out the gentler, more attractive qualities of the personality, which are apt to be smothered by its meticulous sense of order, and its cautious, conservative approach to life.

Comment

This cycle offers further proof of the theory, expressed earlier in this series of comments, that the most productive of all human qualities seems to be intelligence. The factors here include the keen sagacity of the EIGHT — corresponding to the Mercury force in the symbolic pattern — and the constructive, intensive, integrative power of the Saturn frequency, functioning through the creative quality of Water. The personality resulting from this combination should be strong and gentle, just and kindly, clever and sympathetic.

The birthday record of the period includes such names as George Washington, 'Buffalo Bill' Cody, and John Foster Dulles. There are poets in the list: the Chinese Pu-yi, Longfellow, Edna St. Vincent Millay, who shares a birthdate with the composer Fréderic Chopin, and W. H. Auden; songwriter Buffy Sainte-Marie, and songwriter-singer-musician George Harrison. Writer Victor Hugo, and Montaigne, French essayist; as well as John Steinbeck, American novelist. The painter Pierre Auguste Renoir; Ralph Nader, consumer advocate; Meher-Baba, mystic; Johnny Cash, singer; and Zero Mostel, the wild, wonderful comedian, share birthdates in this period. Copernicus was the first Pisces EIGHT on record to change the thinking of the world — he risked his very life for his ideas about the solar system. And Rudolph Steiner, one of the greatest universal geniuses of all times, scientist, artist, architect, educator, philosopher, and seer, adds his brilliance and depth to this cycle's roll of honour.

The list is a varied one, but every name found in it is notable for strength and character — even the poets.

In everyday life, it has been found that this cycle rates a high average of soundness and dependability; the Pisces EIGHTS are naturally well-balanced individuals. Their success in life is apt to be accomplished rather quietly; they do not crave notoriety and fame.

Their greatest weakness is revealed by the name given to the Tarot card — '*Abandoned Success*'. The picture shows a man turning his back on the eight cups that he has apparently piled up with great care, in order to set out across a desert, toward shadowy mountains, in search of something else, some vague, unknown objective. Study of these personalities has revealed that they finish each undertaking with great thoroughness, but are apt to neglect to look ahead and see where it is leading them. This tendency, apparently, arises from their negative habit of getting caught in the web of details and losing the broader vision.

The Pisces EIGHTS have a strong sense of responsibility toward their fellow men, a desire to alleviate suffering, to increase human

'Abandoned Success'

knowledge and intelligence. And, just as long as they remember to keep the sense of humour uppermost, to cultivate laughter and tolerance, they are very apt to leave their world a little better than they found it. George Washington certainly did — and who can measure the achievement of a Pu-yi or a Chopin?

NINE of PISCES

March 1 to 10   (10° to 19°59′ of $\times$)

Potential: NINE   Frequency: JUPITER
(Dependability)   *(Stability)*

Basic Quality: WATER
(Flexibility)

Executive ability, intuition, integrity, and a sense of justice, are combined in this personality. The conflict lies between the practical, logical mind and the intuitive tendency to drift.

On the positive side

There is, in this personality, an intuitive understanding of changing conditions, of cause and effect in human affairs. The Pisces NINES have natural executive ability; they are able to apply their theories and intuitive knowledge to practical affairs with a logical exactness that brings excellent results. They are very patient; they have a keen sense of timing. They know when to wait and when to act. They are generous, friendly, and adaptable — the logic of the Jupiter frequency is softened and balanced by the gentleness of the basic quality and potential, without disturbing the innate equilibrium of the personality. They have a keen appreciation of physical pleasures; they are well equipped to enjoy life and to provide happiness for those about them. They have a keen sense of fair play and justice.

On the negative side

They neglect practical affairs, and get entangled in theories, dreams and illusions. They are always waiting for something they feel is going to happen; they live in a world of unreality, hoping that the next turn of the wheel will be the lucky one. They believe, once they have worked out a satisfactory theory about some enterprise, that the job is done. And when they have a series of disappointments, they work out the theory that they are unlucky — and they believe that, too. They are apt to indulge their physical appetites, sometimes to excess, and such indulgence blunts the fine edge of their natural logic, and slows their mental reactions even more than with the average person. Losing their innate sense of balance and timing, they swing from extreme optimism to utter pessimism. For the wrong-side-out Pisces NINE there is no middle way.

Balance
The habit of logical thinking, and a determination to balance the flashes of intuition — the 'hunches' — by practical analysis and commonsense judgment, is the best way to keep on the positive side, for the Pisces NINES. They have to learn that no theory may be accepted as sound until it has been tested by experience. Temperance in all physical matters, especially eating and drinking, is necessary for these pleasure-loving individuals, but abstentions and prohibitions are not desirable for them. A reasonable discipline, combined with a consistently pragmatic approach to life, both in business and in personal matters, will keep the Pisces NINES on the right track.

Comment
Under normal circumstances, it seems that this personality should be a very fortunate one, and the name of the card suits both the symbols and the people born during the cycle — it is '*Material Happiness*'. Under the disturbed conditions of modern living, however, the Pisces NINES are apt to find it difficult to direct their destinies, so it is natural to find rather a short list of famous names in the period's record of birthdays. It is not easy for these individuals to integrate their abilities and activities into concrete form, and they are much more apt to be retiring than to be ambitious. Unless they are well balanced and completely positive, the Pisces NINES are more interested in their theories than they are in getting results.

They also have a considerable problem in the matter of temperate living. They need, like everyone else, to avoid overindulgence, but severe self-discipline is dangerous for them. The enjoyment they get from physical pleasure is a necessity, not a luxury, for the Pisces NINES. They do their work better, and produce more, when they are not under strict physical regulations, such as diet or fasting. Intemperance, of course, is just as bad as overabstinence for the Pisces NINES. A balance between the two is vitally necessary for their general welfare.

Theorists are in the majority among these persons. Luther Burbank theorized about fruits and vegetables; Paul de Kruif about microbes. Alexander Graham Bell's theories produced that invaluable tool of western life, the telephone; Mircea Eliade investigated and theorized on religions throughout the world, and Pope Pius XII headed one particular branch. The list also includes Bobby Fischer, chessmaster; Dr Seuss, author-artist of zany, wonderful children books; Maurice Ravel, composer; Michelangelo, painter-sculptor-poet; and Elizabeth Barrett Browning, idealistic and romantic poetess.

All NINE potentials induce an independent spirit, but the Jupiter frequency adds a leaning toward order and conventional living that brings an excellent balance to this personality. In spite of their flexibility, and the quiet personal charm that is usually found in their natures, the Pisces NINES have great strength of character. On the

'Material Happiness'

positive side, this appears as reliability, honesty, and a willingness to work. On the negative side, this strength reverts to obstinacy, and a tendency to cling to forlorn hopes. The Tarot document gives them 'a good and generous, though sometimes foolish nature', but credits them with being 'high-minded, not easily satisfied with small and limited ideas'. And it promises them 'complete and perfect realization of pleasure and happiness'.

TEN of PISCES

March 11 to 20   (20° to 29°59′ of X)

Potential: TEN	Frequency: MARS
(Persistence)	*(Activity)*

Basic Quality: WATER
(Flexibility)

Vital energy, personal charm, sensitivity and emotional sympathy are the strong points of this personality. The conflict lies in the opposition between activity and lethargy.

On the positive side

There are definite potentialities for success and achievement in the nature of the Pisces TENS. They are creative, imaginative, and intuitive, with a direct approach to life, tempered by sympathy and human understanding. They are energetic and active, idealistic and constructive, with a strong desire for permanence and perfection. They are friendly, affectionate, generous, and hospitable. They love beauty, pleasure, and happiness, desiring these things more than fame or wealth. They have powerful personal magnetism, being especially attractive to, and attracted by, the opposite sex. They have an instinctive understanding of human problems, and they are very emotional in their human relationships. They are adaptable, gregarious, and usually popular.

On the negative side

They are self-indulgent, impressionable, over-sensitive, and impractical. They follow their personal impulses and desires, obstinately neglecting common sense and consideration for others. They let imagination and instinct govern their actions and reactions, following emotion rather than logic — they let their hearts rule their heads. When negative, they are apt to become fanciful and superstitious, to believe in unrealities and illusions, to be subjective rather than objective, and to lack self-control in relation to physical pleasures and personal emotions.

Balance
Discrimination, self-discipline, and determined objectivity of approach provide the best balance for the Pisces TENS. The positive force of the Mars frequency can be used to balance and direct the flexibility of the Water quality; the persistence of the TEN potential can be directed to constructive ends rather than toward obstructive obstinacy. Always, self-discipline is the key to success and happiness for any Mars frequency, and this is especially true of the Pisces TENS because of their highly charged, dynamic emotional forces, which require an extra measure of direction and control.

Comment
This, the final cycle of the solar year, contains such strong contrasts in its psychological structure that the resultant personalities are often complex, and seemingly contradictory. The vitality and activity of the Mars frequency are sharply opposed to the steady, fundamental persistence of the TEN potential, and neither of these factors is particularly congenial to the gentle flexibility of the Water quality. But — possibly because of its very complexity — the people born during this period are apt to be highly gifted; almost invariably they have a magnetic personal charm that is irresistible, and always they are people who make themselves felt, wherever they are.

An outstanding name in the decanate's birthday record is the great psychic healer, Edgar Cayce. His gentle, beauty-loving personality, his keen, infallible intuitions, and his restorative achievements are typical of the positive potentialities of any Pisces TEN. Another famous psychic medium, Eileen Garrett, was born on March 17, and so, they say, was Saint Patrick. Manly Palmer Hall, renowned occultist and writer; Stephane Malarmé, French symbolist poet meet on this list; as well as Albert Einstein, that kindly, mathematical genius who ironically aided in giving the world a discovery that he later regretted, with all his heart. Among writers we have Henrik Ibsen, Edward

Albee, Philip Roth, and Irving Wallace; also orientalist and adventurer Sir Richard Burton; and psychologist and founder of 'Behaviourism' B. F. Skinner, whose vision of his fellow man illustrates the contradiction and complexity of the psychological structure of this period. We have the legendary dancer Vaslav Nijinsky, and the more contemporary flashing, if not 'flashy' star, Rudolf Nureyev. Jerry Lewis, whose touching characterizations of 'little' people making a zany world even zanier, is also a member of the cycle.

The popular conception of Mars, as a planet or as a mythological figure, is associated with the idea of war; it is said to be a fighting force. Careful study of the symbolic correspondents, however, suggests that like most popular conceptions, this one is not basically correct. The symbols of the Mars force show it to be a creative one, masculine and positive always, destructive or dangerous only when its field is out of balance. This is why self-control seems to be the one best key to success and happiness for any personality having a Mars frequency. The Mars force, in the structure of a personality, expresses itself through the emotions — love, hatred, greed, jealousy,

'Perfected Success'

and the rest — and so requires a very firm hand on the reins.

With the Pisces TENS, it has been found, this emotional control is the thin line between success and failure, happiness and unhappiness — it is vitally necessary to their welfare. Simple self-discipline in the small things, in the details of everyday living, will pay big dividends when it comes to making the larger decisions and putting over the major enterprises — and most of all in the matter of personal happiness, which is what the Pisces TENS really want more than anything else in the world.

PART THREE

1.

THE PRACTICAL USES
OF THE FORMULA

'If we translate salvation into terms of this world, we find that it means achieving harmony between the different parts of our own nature.'
Julian Huxley

If, instead of being a book, this were a Town Meeting, the next item on the programme would be the question period. And — judging from experience — the most urgent of the many questions that might come from all corners of the Town Hall would be: 'How can we *use* this Ten-Day Cycle Formula?'

For, as the reader is probably asking at this moment, what is the good of being aware of the factors of your own birthdate-conditioning, and those of your family and friends, unless you can make some practical application of this knowledge to everyday living? Just where does an understanding of the difference between one basic type, or potential, or frequency, and another, fit into the three main problems of life — work, love, and getting along with other people? What is the actual value of self-knowledge, and the understanding of other people, that can be obtained from the Formula?

There are as many answers to these questions as there are people who will read this book, because — as the Formula shows so clearly — no two individuals will have exactly the same approach to any problem. But it has been found that the frank recognition of the positive and negative factors in the basic structure of your own personality, as outlined in the description of your birthdate cycle, is of considerable help in many practical matters — as, for example, in the making of decisions. Many of our most difficult problems involve a choice of action — 'to be or not to be, that is the question'.

Making a decision, for most of us, is not an easy task, because we have, as a rule, no standard against which to measure our own innate capacities or desires. We do not know what it is that we really want, and so we continue, all through life, making the same mistakes over and over again. This is only one of the ways in which the Formula can be put to work for us — in analyzing our fundamental personal factors in direct relation to the immediate problem, whatever it may be. For, if our decisions can be made in accordance with our natural approach to life, as shown by the basic quality, the potential, and the frequency in each case, it will be more than likely that the decision will be the right one, and will work out to our advantage and satisfaction.

It has been found that the best results are obtained by using the Formula *as a formula*. That is, by taking the various cycle factors as a chemist would take the ingredients of a prescription, and combining them, logically, for application to the purpose or problem in hand — whether the problem is vocational, emotional, or simply a matter of practical decision in everyday affairs.

If, for instance, you belong to the *flexible* type, with a potential of *stability* and an *adaptable* frequency, you will hesitate to undertake a whirlwind campaign of selling, which calls for a dynamic energy and drive that is foreign to your nature. On the other hand, you will undertake with the utmost confidence a constructive, creative job demanding diplomacy and skill in handling people. If, with a potential of *ambition*, you know you have a natural gift for leadership, you will accept responsibilities calling for the exercise of such a gift, knowing that you can depend on your own personal powers to see you through. If you are, by nature, an orderly, quiet worker, interested in doing your job well and thoroughly, getting your personal satisfaction that way rather than by occupying the centre of the stage, you will be much happier if you avoid getting into situations that may demand reactions and responses from you that are contrary to your nature. And so on — the Formula's tabulations of these personal factors, for everyone, are so clear and logical, so fundamental and direct, that their application to any set of circumstances which may arise is not at all a difficult procedure.

From the Formula descriptions of our personal factors, positive and negative, we may learn — by the painless method of self-interested receptivity — the true nature of our own psychological equipment. We begin to understand our own instinctive reactions to good news, bad news, emergencies, responsibilities, and to all the other demands life makes on us from day to day. Instead of blaming ourselves for feeling and acting the way we do, we analyze our own behaviour from a reasonable point of view — we give ourselves a break! Understanding ourselves, we confidently utilize our natural tools and weapons in the accomplishment of our purpose, whatever this may be, from managing the United States Steel Corporation to ordering the dinner.

Most of us are subjected, from childhood up, to invidious comparisons between the way we behave and the way some other person — supposedly superior — would have behaved under similar circumstances. This well-intentioned critical habit of our elders is one of the primary causes for psychology's favourite bogey, the inferiority complex. The strain of trying to live up to someone else's idea of what we ought to be or do is a heavy one, and, as is well known, it often results in the development of a neurosis or psychosis which interferes badly with the individual's efficiency, health, and happiness.

Instead of modelling ourselves according to some artificial standard, the Formula allows us to appraise ourselves fairly and squarely in the light of what might be called an individual standard of our own. It will be noted, in this connection, that the Formula leaves no loopholes for the manufacture of alibis. We are warned always against the dangers of the negative side of the more comfortable virtues such as stability, adaptability, and receptivity. We are told very bluntly that dignity turns wrong side out into a stuffed-shirt type of pride, that active energy degenerates easily into restlessness and recklessness, and that the desire to improve the world around us only too quickly congeals into the lust for personal power.

But we are also told, again and again, throughout the Formula, that by using consistently our positive, natural factors — by being ourselves and keeping right side out — we can make a better job of living than we had believed possible. In the experience of the writer — and this has been corroborated by others who have made a study of individual problems and adjustments — more unhappiness and failure is caused by underestimation and false appraisal of our own capabilities and characteristics than by all our other bad human habits put together. If the Formula can be said to have a purpose, that purpose would be the establishing of a healthy, sane spirit of self-respect throughout the human race.

One of its most interesting functions is that the Formula can be consulted as to why famous people behave the way they do — people whose natures, characteristics, and habits are laid bare to the public view by commentators and biographers, and whose birthdates are generally known. By studying the Formula descriptions of the appropriate cycles, it can be seen how these outstanding personalities have *used* their natural factors, positive, and negative, in attaining notability — or notoriety, as the case may be — and in achieving their own particular form of success or of failure. More can be learned, at times, from a spectacular failure than from a spectacular success, though the process is a less pleasant one.

As noted later, in Chapter 4, many more famous people are found among the SIX potentials than any other. The *peak of fame* period of the year, according to biological research as well as to the Formula, falls in the SIX of Aquarius cycle, running approximately from January 30 to February 9. This phenomenon is explained by the inherent *ambition* of the SIX potential, which induces not only the urge for fame, but also the dignity and charm, the ability for leadership, and the personal magnetism necessary to win and hold a central position on the public stage. It must be recalled, however, that this does not imply that any SIX will automatically attain fame, renown, or leadership. What the Formula shows is that the personal factors natural to every individual born during a cycle with a SIX potential — ambition, charm, dignity, and magnetism — provide the necessary ingredients for the building of a successful leader or public idol.

The desire for power is another human factor that brings individuals into the limelight, but in a different way, and which shows up very clearly in the Formula. Taking Hitler and Mussolini as outstanding examples of the 'power complex', we find that both these world-shattering individuals were born with a FIVE potential, which induces, on its negative side, a desire for personal power and a tendency toward destructive action, and on its positive side, tremendous energy and activity. These two men followed different patterns of dictatorship; Mussolini, in his fight for the power he wanted, kept the Crown and the Church alive in Italy's national structure, while Hitler desired only to destroy everything in his path that might be sacred or traditional. The reason for this vital difference between the two dictators is suggested by the modifying factors of their separate birthdate cycles.

Mussolini's birthdate, July 29, made him a FIVE of Leo. The basic quality of Fire gave him a more positive vitality than Hitler possessed, inducing in Mussolini a steady driving force that rarely weakened. The Saturn frequency of the cycle gave Mussolini a sense of respect for established customs that tended to keep his power complex within bounds, and the combination of factors in his cycle picture endowed Il Duce with a feeling of personal invulnerability which Hitler could never have experienced.

Hitler, born on April 20, was a FIVE of Taurus, having the basic quality of Earth, with a Mercury frequency. In his particular case, the energy of the FIVE potential — which he had chosen to use destructively — was modified only by the keen, surface cleverness of the Mercury frequency, which prefers always not to look too far into the future, but which sees the present with uncanny clarity. This instinctive cunning, with Hitler, was used and directed solely toward getting what he wanted, and what he wanted, as the world soon discovered, was world power. It is interesting to note that the birthdate of Lenin is given as April 21, which gave him the same nucleal psychological factors as Hitler.

This does not mean, of course, that every individual born with a FIVE potential is bound to develop a dictator complex. What the Formula implies here is that in these personalities will be found the basic tendencies that go to make up the nature of an active, strenuous, dominant individual, whose abilities can be used for great good as well as great evil. President Theodore Roosevelt was a FIVE of Scorpio. Elizabeth II is a FIVE of Taurus, and so was William Shakespeare. Carl Jung was a FIVE of Aquarius.

In studying either famous personalities or our own everyday associates in the light of the Formula, it must never be forgotten that no two individuals will use the same set of personal factors in exactly the same way. Illustrating this: suppose a new sporting goods shop presented a set of Jack Nicklaus golf clubs to the first fifty customers who entered their doors. The clubs would be the same in every case, but what a variety of golf games would result, depending on experience, training, and skill! It would be an even bet that not one of the fifty would turn in a Jack Nicklaus score, in spite of the balance and perfection of the clubs.

The factors of any birthdate cycle will be used in an infinite variety of ways by the individuals possessing them — to a more or less successful degree according to the will of the individual. 'Every individuality is definitely perfectible', and the same set of basic personal factors is often found to produce a great artist, a criminal, and a non-entity. But on analysis, the criminal, the artist, and the nonentity are found to be working with the same set of personal tools, driven by the same desires, and showing similar reactions to fundamental tests of character and personality. The people who succeed are found to be the people who make use of their own individual equipment on the positive side and to the best advantage. The people who fail turn out either to be using the negative side of their natures, or trying to live according to some entirely artificial standard that is out of tune with their natural psychological equipment.

Thus, it can be seen, the Formula adds considerable interest to the reading of history and biography, as well as to the understanding of current news and happenings. The course of events is directly affected by the personalities who are pulling the strings and directing the activities of the world. One example of this will suffice: the extraordinary change in the public spirit of war-time England when Neville Chamberlain, a TEN of Pisces, gave place to Winston Churchill, an EIGHT of Sagittarius, while Hitler was thundering at the gates of London. There could hardly have been a greater contrast between two personalities. Chamberlain, having the persistent conservatism of a TEN potential, the receptive flexibility of the basic quality of Water, and the emotional instability of a Mars frequency, was unfitted by nature to cope with the cunning power complex of Hitler, with his Mercury frequency, his FIVE potential, and his hard basic quality of Earth. But Winston Churchill brought into the picture the dynamic energy of Fire, plus the doubled sagacity and ability for swift, direct action of the EIGHT potential, and a Mercury frequency, more powerful than Hitler's because of its basic energy.

The whole world watched, in the summer of 1940, while Churchill turned the tide of England's morale, inspiring his country with his own fiery enthusiasm, and rousing the British Lion to roaring and lashing its tail in proper British fashion.

Examples of this kind turn up in the news almost every day, and as we discover how strongly events and conditions are influenced by personalities, the better we can understand what is going on around us, both in the broad perspective of the world at large and in the immediate environment of our own personal lives.

The Formula is perhaps most useful of all in the understanding of our own close associates — those to whom we are so linked by circumstances that a perspective is difficult to achieve. The old saying that 'love is blind' is only too true; any emotional relationship between two people is apt to prejudice personal judgment. In the next chapter, this subject of personal relationships as analyzed by the Formula is dealt with very fully and here it will be referred to only briefly.

The closest and most difficult of all human relationships are, of course, the marital and the parental. Between husband and wife, or between parents and children, the friction which arises can be the cause of great unhappiness, often of the ruin of more lives than one. An impersonal viewpoint, in these cases, is almost impossible to attain. The Formula's analysis of each individual, and of the basic factors of relationship between them, provides a practical, scientific viewpoint from which adjustments can be made.

Practical experience has shown this to be true. Only a few marriages, on the average, take place between people who are 'affinities' according to the Formula, and for the many others, a clear understanding of the personal factors involved makes for an increase of tolerance and mutual respect — which is an excellent foundation for the endurance of love and affection. The dynamic emotional wife comes to accept her practical husband as a dependable running mate, and the husband enjoys the stimulus of her enthusiasm and energy without being driven or disturbed by it. Each one learns what to expect — and what not to expect — from the other, without hard feelings and criticism entering into the picture. If the wife happens to be the gentler and more receptive member of the partnership, she is reminded by the Formula analysis of her own cycle not be become a doormat for the dynamic, over-positive husband to trample upon — and also, to allow him plenty of scope for the exercise of his own energies. This particular type of combination is one that is apt to produce too much practice of the gentle art of nagging, that prime destroyer of happy marriages.

Most subtle of all marital adjustments, it has been found, comes when one or both the partners in the marriage belong to the mental type, with the basic quality of Air. To make personal, emotional adjustments on an impersonal, mental level is not easy — until the power of the mental factors, as weapons, can be recognized and skillfully used. Here, the Formula analysis of each individual cycle can be of invaluable assistance in making the adjustment, particularly when the factors of relationship as outlined in Chapter 2 are taken into consideration.

The frequent friction between parents and children is found to be based not on the difference of a generation — which is usually given the blame — but on the definite lack of understanding between one individual and another. Parents rather often indulge in the habit of expecting their children to be exact reproductions of themselves; they feel almost aggrieved when their offspring show evidence of specialized individualism. This is one of the most familiar foundations for family misunderstandings; it is apt to create rifts between parent and child at critical periods of the relationship, thus destroying its beauty and value in the lives of both of them, as well as undermining the family harmony.

Here again the clear-cut analysis found in the Formula's descriptions of the appropriate birthdate cycles has been found to be of real and lasting value. Not only is the parent enabled to understand the child, but the child, when old enough, to understand both parents, from an impersonal and unemotional point of view. There is created in the family, through such understanding, a sense of mutual respect, the lack of which is so often the principal cause of discord in the home. So many examples have come under the writer's notice that several volumes of case histories would be required to cover them. Every problem of personal relationships is different from every other, and must be worked out according to the many factors involved. But to work out any problem, a logical starting point is required. In all questions involving personalities, the Formula supplies a starting point which is logical and surprisingly accurate. And, of all the problems and questions we face from day to day, how many are there which do *not* involve personalities? Coming right down to cases, it is found that there are none.

Any practical problem demands both the clear understanding of our own motives, desires, and personal capacities, and those of some other individual or group of individuals with whom we happen to be dealing. With this understanding as a starting point, or platform, the approach to almost any undertaking that can be imagined is greatly simplified. To begin with, when we understand the people with whom we must co-operate, we can modify our personal approach to them accordingly. We do not try to bully a SIX, or to drive a SEVEN. We respect the slow-functioning mind of the orderly FOUR, and the indecision of the TWO. We present only practical details to an EIGHT, only the fundamental points of any question to a NINE, and we deal very warily with the overbearing persistence of a TEN.

We appeal to the emotions of the FIRE quality, to the creative imagination of the WATER quality, to the logic of the AIR quality, or to the practical sense of the EARTH quality in the individuals with whom we are working.

And, at all times, we adjust the subtlety of our approach to our friends and associates according to our best understanding of our own natures, and of how our personalities can best co-operate with theirs.

2.
GETTING ALONG TOGETHER

'I do not like thee, Dr Fell,
The reason why, I cannot tell.'

'Everyone is a little queer but thee and
me — and even thee is a little queer!'

During the evolution of the Ten-Day Cycle Formula, one of the most interesting developments to emerge was a pattern of personal relationships — harmonious and otherwise — between one individual and another. As personal relationships are admittedly the outstanding human problem, this aspect of the birthdate formula is of particular interest. Nine-tenths of all our conversation is concerned with the subject of how people are getting along together — from neighbourhood gossip to formal discussions of international situations. And, as a rule, we confess to being puzzled.

While the Formula offers no magical solution for world peace or family harmony, it serves an interesting and practical purpose in the very vital matters of loving and hating, congeniality and discord, affinity and antipathy between individuals. It does not dispose of our personal relationship problems, but it gives us a workable basis for understanding them — family feuds, parental difficulties, marital troubles, simple friendships and enmities, and business associations. And there can be no doubt that understanding is the first essential to the better handling of any personal situation in the world.

Perhaps the primary difficulty in personal relationships is that we are apt to judge everyone else by our own standards — we measure other people according to our individual personal characteristics. '*Even thee is a little queer!*' The Formula reminds us that there are many different approaches to life besides our own. Not only this, it tells us what these various approaches are, according to the birthdate-conditioning factors of each individual concerned. Even without the specific suggestions that are given here of natural congeniality or discord existing between certain basic qualities, potentials, and frequencies, the mere clarification of the vagaries of the human family as a whole — which the Formula itself provides — would be a practical contribution toward better human relationships.

In applying the Formula to a personal relationship problem, it has been found that the best results can be obtained by using the Formula impersonally — that is, by studying the fundamental factors of each personal structure, much as a scientist would observe the working out of an experiment. The three factors — basic quality, potential, and frequency — in their common sense relationship to each other from one personality to another, can be examined unemotionally and critically. In this way, adjustments can be made with greater speed and less embarrassment than is possible with certain other methods such as psychoanalysis or technical questionnaires. Using the Formula, it is possible to achieve an impersonal viewpoint, which is usually rather difficult where personal matters are concerned.

The almost infinite variations of the human psychological pattern suggest, of course, that any kind of statistical report on the subject of human relationships would be both absurd and misleading. The factors involved are too subtle to lend themselves to statistical study. The Formula's tabulation of affinities and antipathies is nothing more than an orderly structure on which can be built a broad, practical understanding of the basic relationship between one person and another, according to the individual factors involved — the basic quality, the potential, and, to a lesser degree, the frequency, in each case. While considerable research remains to be done in this field, the results to date, in personal happiness and adjustment, have been sufficiently productive to warrant setting forth the structure of the relationship pattern here.

While ordinary judgment has to be used in every case, there are certain fundamentals clearly stated in the sources of the Formula, and others which have shown themselves in practice. Even though it is manifestly impossible to condense the many angles of application within the limits of a single chapter, it is hoped that by now the reader is sufficiently familiar with the Formula methods to analyze the factors that are present in each case, and to carry the analysis just one step further. Instead of concentrating on the under-standing of *one* individual in relation to life in general, *two* personalities are studied in their relation to each other.

The fundamentals of the affinity pattern are given here, beginning with the most obvious and the most important of the relationships — that which lies between the BASIC QUALITIES of any two individuals.

The basic qualities

Just as the basic qualities — symbolized by the four original 'elements' of FIRE, AIR, WATER, and EARTH — form the foundation of the personality structure in the Formula, so they provide the fundamental factors in the pattern of relationships. While the specific harmony or discord between the types is modified somewhat by contradictory relationships of potential or frequency, the basic type relationships are found to be remarkably consistent. They conform with startling accuracy to an ancient postulate set forth by the unknown recorders of the source document — the Tarot document — which divides the four 'elements' into *friendly* and *unfriendly* categories with clear-cut simplicity, thus:

> FIRE is friendly with AIR, unfriendly to EARTH and WATER
> AIR is friendly with FIRE, unfriendly to WATER and EARTH
> WATER is friendly with EARTH, unfriendly to AIR and FIRE
> EARTH is friendly with WATER, unfriendly to FIRE and AIR

This tabulation sounds rather like some sort of alchemical abracadabra, but it turns out to have a very special basis in fact, especially in relation to that closest and most critical of all human relationships — marriage. A careful study of many marriage relationships has shown that the happiest and most enduring marriages usually take place between people whose basic qualities of birthdate-conditioning correspond to the *friendly* categories of the ancient tabulation.

That is — in the language of the Formula — it seems that within the complexities of our various individualities, the basic qualities of *practical sense* in one person will have an affinity for the qualities of *flexibility* in someone else. The same thing is true of *dynamic energy* in relation to *mentality*; these combinations 'click', and tend to induce that subtle and mysterious link between a man and woman which creates a lasting bond.

In the interpretation and translation of the ancient symbols, it has developed that the best way to discover their true meaning, as a rule, is to take that meaning as literally as possible. So, while fire and water, in their familiar forms of flame and liquid have nothing to do with the case — which is quite obvious — it is intriguing to discover that the discordant relationship between the basic qualities so symbolized is that the WATER quality is found to have a *quenching* effect on the FIRE quality in individuals. Conversely, the FIRE personality is apt to have a stimulating, disturbing and *over-heating* effect on the gentler individual having the WATER quality — sometimes to the point of exhaustion, as if the pot had boiled dry. Whereas, in the 'friendly' combination symbolized by FIRE and AIR, it is easy to see that actual fire and air are mutually inter-dependable, feeding one another with just the necessary qualities for the steady glowing of the flame. It is in this fashion that symbolic statements can be interpreted and translated for clear understanding. They are always logical, simple, and practical.

Visualizing actual earth and water with the same lucidity, we remember at once that seeds grow in the earth only by the help of water, and also that water can only be productive when in contact with earth. Air, in itself, in relation to earth, produces nothing better than dust, and fire only dries and cracks the earth, destroying fertility. The ancient wise men, in their use of symbols, were uncannily exact. There could hardly be a more graphic description of the interplay of personalities as it works out in actual life than this quaint postulate of friendly and unfriendly 'elements' in the basic qualities of the individuals concerned, according to their birthdate-conditioning.

It is easy to see how dynamic energy, as a personal quality, needs the balance of discrimination and clear thinking — FIRE and AIR. Hard, practical sense calls for the humanizing effects of flexibility, as with EARTH and WATER. Thinkers feel the need of dynamic co-operators to drive them from theory to action, which FIRE can do for AIR, while the dreamy folk — the WATER people — require just the kind of prodding that can be administered by the practical force of EARTH. The ancient postulate works out with considerable logic.

It seems, too, that people who are basically complementary to each other will be less likely to get in each other's way than people who are too much alike, or who are fundamentally at odds with one another. Many a bitter quarrel is nothing more than the unconscious protest of one basic quality against the restriction, domination, or sheer incompatibility of another — again, like water quenching fire, fire burning up earth, or earth trying vainly to bring forth fruit in response to the cool, unfertilizing breath of air.

But of course, as is quite obvious, the pattern of human relationships is not so simple in design that we can segregate ourselves tidily into four separate packets and have done with it. Something of the endless complexity that we perceive in our tangled relationships appears in the Formula when we add to the basic qualities those other two factors in the human pattern, the potentials and frequencies, with their varied possibilities of mutual harmony and discord. And here again we are rescued from a too bewildering complexity by the orderly arrangement of the symbols themselves, with their fundamental meanings.

The potentials

With the potentials — symbolized by the numbers — a simple harmonic law of some kind seems to be at work in the pattern. It may be that an omniscient mathematician will supply, one day, the reason for the surprising fact that the most harmonious relationship between the potentials appears to be, in the Formula, *the interval of three* — as, a Four with a Seven, a Five with an Eight, and so on — particularly when the basic qualities in the case conform to the 'friendly' postulate stated on the previous page, which creates the affinity tabulation.

As with the basic qualities, the potential relationships seem to imply complementary factors. The versatility of the Seven, for example, is balanced and steadied by the stability of the Four, or by the persistence and conservatism of the Ten — while the Ten and Four receive, in return, from the Seven, the necessary stimulation and enlivening to keep them from dullness and from stodginess.

Again, the restless activity of the Five is kept in check by the sagacity and clear vision of the Eight, and receives the needed gift of harmonious balance from the adaptability of the Two. In its turn, the Five is naturally stimulating to the restrictive sense of the Eight and the uncertainty of the Two.

The fixed pride and ambition of the Sixes can be mobilized effectively by the intensity of the Three or by the forcefulness of the Nine, while the Six produces a focus, or balancing point, for the sometimes overpositive forces of the Three or Nine. From this brief analysis, it can be seen that the affinity pattern provides, in each case, complementary *positive* factors to offset the *negative* factors of the individuals concerned, which certainly seems to be an excellent arrangement.

Similar potentials are found to be congenial, but unproductive. An interval of *one*, or *two*, between potentials makes for friendliness and comradeship, but not for warm affection. An interval of *four* creates mutual respect, but an interval of *five* nearly always produces mutual discord. The interval of *six* provides the closest approximation to affinity, but does not quite achieve it, while the interval of *seven* is again discordant. The interval of *eight* is apparently so impersonal that it creates neither harmony nor discord between individuals.

The frequencies

Being the most subtle factors in the Formula pattern, the frequencies — symbolized by the planetary names — are less susceptible to logical analysis than are the basic qualities and the potentials. The frequencies are somehow elusive, having a will-o'-the-wisp enchantment that leads the would-be analyst over endless fields of speculation. There can be little doubt, however, that the frequencies were named, not for the planets, but for the gods of ancient mythology, at a time when every deity represented a simple, human emotion.

It seems that the frequencies are nearer to the surface of personality than the other two factors, and therefore are subject to an even greater variety of expression in their modification of an individuality. It follows that in their combinations, through personal relationships, there are so many possibilities of harmony and discord that even the mathematician's *googol* would fail to compass them. However, as always, by studying their basic meanings, as symbols, in the structure of the Formula, we are able to deduce a reasonable amount of useful information as to their application in the matter of human relationships.

No one knows who first gave to the Saturn symbol its psychological qualification of sternness and discipline, but living at close quarters with anyone having a Saturn frequency in the birthdate pattern provides convincing evidence of its truth. There is another side to his stern frequency: a protective, kindly quality that shows itself, in personal relationships, as the soft spot in the Saturn individual. Noting this, we recall that mythology gives many names to Saturn, among them *Kronos*, meaning *time*, and that we speak familiarly of *Father Time*, visualizing a stern but compassionate old gentleman with long whiskers and a scythe. It is not surprising, therefore, to find in the Saturn frequency, as related to other frequencies, a fatherly kindness as well as seriousness and a keen sense of responsibility. This characteristic, naturally, has a steadying effect on the Venus versatility, the Mars impetuosity, or the Moon instability, whereas in combination with the Sun, both natures are too intense for mutual happiness. Combined with Jupiter, the Saturn frequency is mentally congenial, so it follows that this combination would work out better, as a rule, in practical business relationships than in the closer personal associations.

It seems that there is no actual affinity pattern among the frequencies. Every frequency, taken from the point of view of its own factors, will blend — with varying success — in relationships with any other. It is logical to expect, for instance, that Mars and Venus, in mythology the male and female deities of physical passion, will have an affinity for one another. But after studying their several characteristics — the versatile, undependable nature of Venus and the restless, combative activity of Mars — we would hardly look for a peaceful union between them, and this is rarely found. The dignity of the Sun and the stability of the Jupiter frequency obviously would not combine to produce a happy relationship, as both frequencies are too static in their emotional approach, and the result is apt to be a stalemate. Mars gets along much better, as a friendly frequency, with either Jupiter or Sun frequencies, than they do with one another, and the same thing is true of the more volatile Venus and Moon frequencies.

But Mars and Moon frequencies, both being unstable in different ways, are basically at odds with one another. It is interesting to note that in the table of affinities, which shows the most harmonious relationships possible to the human family, according to the Formula, certain frequency combinations are never found: Mars and Moon, Sun and Saturn, Sun and Moon, Jupiter and Venus, Jupiter and Mercury, Saturn and Venus do *not* appear as affinities anywhere within the tabulation. Mercury, being the most impersonal of all the frequencies, is the most difficult to understand in matters of human relationship, especially the closer ties, marriage, family, and parental.

It is apparent, however, that the frequency relationships are the least arbitrary of the three, and allow a greater latitude of adjustment between individuals. If science can discover just what part the frequencies actually play in the field of the earth and of individuals, a closer analysis of their interrelationship will be possible. At present, they remain a mystery of the 'four-dimensional time-space continuum' of quanta physics, the only clue to their psychological meaning and application being found in Keightley's immortal volume on classical mythology.

While this pattern of relationship would seem to be arbitrary in its general structure, it is actually anything but arbitrary in its indications of happy or unhappy, successful or disastrous relations between individuals. Like the direct personal application of the Formula, the relationship pattern is encouraging and hopeful, as it suggests that through a better understanding of the factors in each individual, and their various complementary values, as well as their definite points of possible discord, personal adjustments can be made even between people who have great trouble in getting on together, and whose individual birthdate factors fall far short of complying with the rules of harmony set out in the Formula pattern of affinities.

In addition to the tabulated affinity relationships, it stands to reason that many other combinations will be congenial, in varying degrees. For example, two people having similar qualities, potentials, or frequencies in their birthdate patterns will understand each other fairly well because their approach to life, in one respect at least, will be the same. Similarity is a less likely creator of discord than is a conflict of inharmonious factors, especially if the basis of such a similarity is understood and appreciated, in relation to the other factors involved in both the birthdate patterns in question. No exact definitions can be laid down, of course, in this. Just as 'every individuality is indefinitely perfectible', so every relationship between individuals can be adjusted, if not to perfection, at least to considerable improvement in happiness of co-operation.

The real value of the Formula's affinity pattern seems to lie in the fact that it provides a basis of understanding relating to those inexplicable affinities and antipathies that spring up between people in everyday life. It offers a possible explanation for the passionate loves and hatreds that so often exist between people for no apparent reason, and also the fact that people who may be outwardly uncongenial, having widely different tastes, habits and training, so frequently get along unexpectedly well, either in casual or close relationships. It may be that the Formula provides a key to that ancient bug-bear of biology, the age-old mystery of natural selection, and that if we knew the birthdates of history's great lovers, Dante and Beatrice, Romeo and Juliet, Anthony and Cleopatra, Aucassin and Nicolette, we might find a clue to the magical attraction between them.

Be that as it may, the affinity pattern of relationships is evidently a part of the broad psychological scheme set forth in the Formula. It has, as its only possible objective, the increasing of human happiness — the sharpening of individual skill in the pursuit of destiny. It can be applied to the best practical purposes by studying, through the knowledge of their birthdate factors in relation to our own, those people we live with and work with, love and hate, admire and fear, and who, in almost every case, we fail to understand.

3.

NOTHING BUT A PACK OF CARDS

'The dynamism of cards is beyond all discussion; one does not argue about it; one undergoes it. This thin bundle of pasteboard strips which is shuffled over a table is for some the instrument of ruin . . . for others, a mysterious door opening on a gaping and unfathomable future of illusions and hopes. Taking everything into account, the strange power of this collection of rude, archaic pictures, which leads from Bridge to the Kabala, from Poker to the science of Hermes, and from Baccarat to the Ain-Soph, deserves to be the object of our serious thought and study.'

Grillot de Givry

'Who cares for you?' said Alice. (She had grown to her full size by this time.) 'You're nothing but a pack of cards!'

Lewis Carroll

One of the few remaining historical mysteries is the origin and significance of the pack of cards. No one knows who invented playing cards, when and where the pack was first constructed, or for what purpose, though a number of volumes have been filled with conjecture on these points. It is generally accepted, however, that the pack we use today for poker and bridge — and fortune-telling — is directly descended from the European pack known as the 'Tarot', which is believed to be of medieval origin.

This ancient pack, whose spot-cards play such an important role in the Ten-Day Cycle Formula, has been surrounded by certain writers with an aura of mystery that has somewhat discouraged practical research into its history and possible origin. It now appears, however, that one of the 'occult' legends associated with the invention of the Tarot pack — and therefore of the modern pack of cards, its lineal descendant — throws considerable light upon the mystery. Not only does this legend accord with certain historical facts, but it offers an explanation of the seemingly fantastic link between the structure of a pack of cards and the course of the solar year — thus giving the cards a more reasonable place in the Formula picture than would otherwise be possible. Cards have always had for us a touch of magic; something just a trifle uncanny, out of the ordinary. This legend, which until now has been jealously guarded by 'occultists' and — as a result — scorned by historians, offers a certain clarification of the mystery of the pack of cards itself, and also of the sources of the Ten-Day Cycle Formula.

The Tarot legend takes us back to the time when the Dark Ages were merging into the Middle Ages — as we view it today. It is probable that from the viewpoint of the period itself, the Dark Ages were at their darkest, with little hope of returning sanity in a barbaric world. We have to remember, too, that this legend refers to a time when scholars, the scientists of the period, assumed and accepted a universal order in the scheme of things, in which man was included without question. This scientific approach, however, was under the ban of the early Christian Church. According to Tertullian, and other ecclesiastical writers, the early Christians regarded all of the arts, the sciences, and literature, as tools of the devil. The ecclesiastical authorities — we would call them dictators today — destroyed all records of the earlier cultures; they closed the colleges of learning in Athens and Alexandria; they burned the libraries. These facts are well known, and history shows that the Church was helped along in its totalitarian efforts by frequent waves of barbaric invasions, which swept over one country after another, leaving complete destruction in their wake. One writer describes this process as 'an intellectual mortuary veil, the black wave of barbarism that during the Middle Ages came nigh to wiping out all traces of civilization.' [1]

The legend states that in or around the year 1200, a small group of learned men met secretly in the Moroccan city of Fez, which was one of the few remaining outposts of culture in the dying civilization of the time. Even in Fez, at the beginning of the 13th century, the intellectual blackout was closing in rapidly. We read, in *The Seven Seals of Science*, that 'the chief accomplishments of the Arabs in Spain as elsewhere was to keep the torch of science alight until Christian Europe was ready to receive it, but their creative effort had spent itself completely by the middle of the 12th century.'[2] Our legend — which thus seems to be correctly timed — relates that the few surviving scholars of the period were holding, at the beginning of the 13th century, what today would be called a Convention for the Preservation of Science. They had gathered together in Fez to discuss ways and means of putting on record, in some fashion, certain important knowledge that they believed should be conserved for future generations. This record, obviously, must be put in a form that would rouse neither the suspicion of the Christians nor the destructive ferocity of the barbarians.

After considerable discussion, it seems, the learned men agreed upon a plan. The knowledge that they wished to put on record could not be written in plain words, as all literature save Holy Writ was under the ban of ecclesiastical totalitarianism. Symbols, too, were included in the ban — mathematical, alchemical, and astronomical alike. Only two things were left: pictures, and numbers. In one of the very few printed records of this legend the author tells us that the wise men 'hit upon the device of embodying the most important of their doctrines in a book of pictures, whose combinations should depend upon the occult harmonies of numbers'. And further, that 'as a skeleton for their invention the wise men chose the simple system of numbers and letters afforded by the Kabala, or Secret Wisdom of Israel.'[3]

The Tarot pack is the only 'book of pictures' remaining to us from medieval times that in any way answers to the description given in the legend. The 'simple system of numbers' in the Kabala is found to be a combination of *four* and *ten*: the four holy letters of the Name of God, and the ten branches on the Tree of Life. So it seems that a pack of cards having *four* suits, each suit containing a numbered series of cards from one to *ten*, and with *four* court cards — King, Queen, Prince and Princess — answers the Kabalistic requirements of the story rather well. Historically, the legend would seem to receive some support from the official report on the history and origin of playing cards, prepared for the British Museum by W. H. Willshire, which covers the available facts more thoroughly than any other discoverable record.

In the Museum's report, the time of the origin of the pack of cards narrows down to the very early 13th century, and the place is generally accepted as being in Spain. One of the earliest known references to playing cards — says the report — is a statement by the Abbe de la Rive, an accredited historian of the Renaissance, that cards were brought to Italy from Spain when the Spaniards entered Sicily and Calabria under the Castilian princes, in the year 1267. Mr Willshire makes two comments which are of particular interest in connection with the present research and the Ten-Day Cycle Formula. On page 7, he writes: 'There is no satisfactory evidence that cards were ever anything else than of European origin.' And on page 21, after a thorough sifting of the evidence, Mr Willshire adds: 'Careful research has proved, we think, that at first all the card germs were purely emblematic in character, and intended for instructive diversion.'[4]

'Instructive diversion' suggests that the original form of the pack of cards was decidedly not for purposes of gambling, but rather for teaching or study. Other legends, so far unauthenticated, report that the Tarot pack was turned over to the Gypsies by the wise men of Fez, for safekeeping — as no one would suspect a fortunetelling Gypsy of being intellectual! The only difficulty here is that the Gypsies do not appear in European history until much later, which tends to spoil the story. What seems more likely is that the correlation between the pack of cards and the course of time was known, and deliberately used by skilful soothsayers for predictive purposes, and thus the whole tradition of fortunetelling by cards was started and built up, to be used by all fortunetellers down through history, the Gypsies included.

It seems that the structure of the Tarot pack has been very little changed since its earliest known appearance in the 13th century. With only slight differences, such as the suit names,[5] and the dropping of the fourth court card, the Princess, the standard pack in use today is modelled on the original of the Tarot. In its present available form, the Tarot pack itself includes an additional series of twenty-two extra cards, known as 'major trumps' or 'keys'. These cards are known by their traditional titles, which vary slightly in different versions and translations, but remain consistent with their earliest known connotations.[6] The twenty-two keys are probably not a part of the original pack; this is stated definitely by Grillot de Givry, in contradiction to many other commentators on the subject, and it seems to the present writer that de Givry's idea is the more logical one. He says that the four suit pack is undoubtedly 'of more ancient origin than the twenty-two mysterious figures, upon which one is generally impelled, because of their very mystery, to confer the reputation of greater antiquity'.[7] Most of the available commentaries on the Tarot pack are devoted almost entirely to an attempted explanation of the 'keys' and pay very little attention to the suit cards except to point out, with complete unanimity, that the four suits are attributed to the four ancient 'elements', Fire, Water, Air, and Earth. The source document of the Formula, as will be seen, takes the opposite viewpoint, and gives the position of major importance to the suit cards.

Two of the most popular illusions about the Tarot pack have been its alleged Egyptian origin — which apparently was fabricated by a philologist of the 18th century, Court de Gebelin, who has been found to be a writer of lively imagination rather than a historian — and its supposed invention by a French painter at the court of Charles VI of France. The French origin theory is based on a single, and doubtless correct entry in a court ledger of the year 1392, referring to 'three packs of cards in gold and divers colours' painted 'for the king's diversion' by an artist named Gringonneur.[7] Both these rumours are disposed of by the official report of the British Museum, quoted above, which ends with a long excerpt from *The History of Transcendental Magic* by Eliphas Levi, a famous French Kabalist of the 19th century. The excerpt includes the following, in Levi's best melodramatic style:

'When the Sovereign Priesthood ceased in Israel, when all the oracles of the world became silent in the presence of the Word become Man and speaking by the mouth of the most popular and gentlest of sages . . . the mysteries of the Ephod and the Teraphim, no longer recorded on gold and precious stones, were written, *or rather figured*, by certain wise Kabalists, first on ivory, parchment, or gilt, and afterwards on simple cards which were always objects of suspicion to the official Church as containing a dangerous Key to its mysteries.'[8]

Another interesting and pertinent angle of the Tarot legend is its reference to the meeting of the wise men at Fez as being 'secret'. There is a persistent tradition, found in many medieval and eighteenth-century writings, that much of the 'secret knowledge' of the 'ancient wisdom' has been preserved by being handed down, from generation to generation, through the members of secret orders, groups who were bound by strict vows to keep their knowledge from the public — or, as they styled it, from the profane. Undoubtedly this tradition arose simply enough from the persecution of scientists and scholars by the early Church, during the Dark Ages, and was later hedged round with mystery by charlatans — who appear in any generation — for purposes of gain. The entire hocus-pocus of 'occultism' seems to have stemmed from the historical fact of the Church's persecution of scholarship, which was carried out for the purpose of gaining political power. But the idea of secrecy has such undying charm that even in the beginning of the 20th century we find one of these 'secret orders' functioning in England under the name of 'The Order of the Golden Dawn'. Early in the century, it seems, there came a breakup in this Order, and some of the rebellious members got together and published a considerable number of the Order's private papers. It was among the pages of this publication[9] that the description of the Tarot pack, with the ten-day cycle attributions and symbols, was found.

The connection between the 'Order of the Golden Dawn' in 20th-century London and the Convention for the Preservation of Science in 13th-century Fez is thus not as farfetched as it might appear. The 'Golden Dawn' is said to be one of the secret orders of the old tradition, and its history and papers, which are now available in book form,[10] make very interesting reading for anyone who wishes to pursue the subject further. As far as the Ten-Day Cycle Formula is concerned, however, the only document of pertinent interest is the description of the Tarot pack, which is included in a long and complicated series of papers entitled 'BOOK T'.

At first reading, the entire document appears to be set forth in the usual unintelligible gibberish of the average 'occult' work, and to have no practical significance whatever. In the course of any research job, however, the worker is always looking for clues; in this case, for a clue to the qualities of time. So it was that upon more serious examination of BOOK T, several significant features appeared in the *description of the cards of the Tarot, with their attributions*.

To begin with, the order in which the cards are described is most peculiar. The suits are not followed through in their logical sequence, as might be expected, and the twenty-two keys, which usually take precedence in any Tarot commentary, are briefly described at the end of the document. First come the four Aces, described as a separate unit. Next, in a section by themselves, are found descriptions of the sixteen court cards. Following this, again quite separately, follow 'the descriptions of the smaller cards of the four suits, thirty-six in number, answering unto the thirty-six Decans of the Zodiac'. The 'Decan' being the traditional name for the ten-day cycle, there is no possible doubt as to the intended correlation between the spot-cards and the cycles. Such a correlation appeared to be quite meaningless until certain other curious details were observed. One of these was the fact that the spot-cards, instead of being described in their normal sequence, one complete suit at a time, swing back and forth between the suits, thus following the order, not of the pack, but of the solar year. It is as if the cards had been deliberately laid out in the pattern of the year.

Another factor causing the spot-card descriptions to stand out from the rest was their form of expression, which differs sharply from the balance of the document. An 'occult' work is never easy reading, whether the reader is trying to make sense out of it or merely indulging in a metaphysical orgy. In this case, the usual vague and windy phrases are found in the descriptions of the 22 keys, the Aces, and the court cards. But when it comes to the description of the spot-cards the document abruptly changes its approach, and begins to employ terms that suggest, unmistakably, psychological factors. [11]

This contrast in terms was one of the first evidences to appear that a formula of psychological time factors (qualities of time, as Jung called them) might lie hidden behind the archaic, symbolic, but logical and direct phrases of the spot-card descriptions. When the accompanying symbols were fully analyzed according to their basic meanings — that is, meanings which are generally accepted among symbolists of all creeds and schools — the psychological significance of the Ten-Day Cycle card descriptions appeared with dramatic clarity. And, as the research developed, it became more and more evident that these thirty-six sections of the document, supposedly applicable only to the Tarot cards themselves, were really a series of clear-cut personality portraits, descriptive of all individuals born during each specific ten-day time cycle. The average of accuracy, under reasonable test, was too high to allow for any doubt on this point.

The present research suggests that in constructing the original Tarot pack, the wise men of Fez were making a glyph, or composite symbol, of the interrelated forces at work in the world we live in, as they understood them at the time. They were also recording their conviction — as shown by the accuracy of the Formula — that mankind is definitely a part of the universal order of things. According to the science of antiquity, everything could be analyzed under the four fundamental classifications of Fire, Water, Air, and Earth, and the structure of the pack faithfully mirrors this postulate in the four suits.

This idea of the fourfold structure of the universe was considered by the ancients to be a hypothesis of great significance. It appears in all the older philosophies, and was undoubtedly the underlying principle of the cross as a universal symbol — the symbol being, of course, much older than Christianity. It appears in the form of a crude swastika on a very ancient Mayan tablet, uncovered in Mexico, and was evidently, even in Mayan times, a sacred symbol. [12] One interesting point about this Mayan cross, in relation to the present research, is that the four arms of the cross are of varying lengths, as if to emphasize a difference between them. All sacred symbolism runs to *fours* — Ezekiel, in the Old Testament, gives great importance to the symbol of the 'Four Beasts': the Lion, Eagle, Bull, and Man. In the New Testament we find the four Evangels, and everyone who has investigated the fascinating subject of angels knows that four Archangels stand at the head of the heavenly hierarchy — Michael, Gabriel, Raphael, and Uriel. The number four is somehow inescapable: we have four seasons, four winds, and four beats to the rhythm of a march-tune. Last, but not least, we have four suits in the pack of cards. The single abortive effort, made not long ago, to introduce a fifth suit into the bridge pack, was a dismal failure. In the light of the apparent relationship between the structure of the pack and the solar year, such an effort would seem rather like an attempt to change the course of nature — which, as everybody knows, cannot be done!

Is the pack of cards, then, a composite psychological blueprint of the human family, in terms of the changing cycles of the solar year? Such an idea is, of course, so contrary to all accepted theories that it seems closer to fantasy than to fact. But the accuracy of the Ten-Day Cycle Formula, which without the Tarot pack would never have been formulated, suggests that Alice may have been right after all when she said to the human race in general — just as she regained her normal stature after her adventures in Wonderland — '*you're nothing but a pack of cards!*'

The idea is far from discouraging. For, if the wise men of Fez thought so highly of their understanding of the human family as an orderly, harmonious structure — at a time when human vandalism was rapidly destroying all evidence that mankind was anything more than a rapacious beast — that they took the trouble to fashion this ingenious and indestructible record for succeeding generations to decipher, perhaps humanity is better than it sometimes seems. Our self-respect as human beings can be considerably increased by the discovery that the psychological structure of human individuality was the one thing the wise men sought to save out of the wreckage of the Dark Ages, even as our sense of humour is tickled at the thought of the hiding place they chose for its protection.

Notes

1. *Queen Moo and the Egyptian Sphinx* by Augustus le Plongeon. Published by the author (page xv).
2. *Seven Seals of Science* by Joseph Mayer. Century Company, 1927 (page 51).
3. *Brief Analysis of the Tarot* by Paul Foster Case. Ellicott Press, Buffalo, 1927 (page 2).
4. British Museum Catalogue of Playing Cards, 1776, Section I, page 21.
5. The old names of the suits were WANDS, CUPS, SWORDS, and PENTACLES, for CLUBS, HEARTS, SPADES, and DIAMONDS in the order given.
6. The titles of the twenty-two keys are: The Fool, The Magician, The High Priestess, The Empress, The Emperor, The Hierophant, The Lovers, The Chariot, Strength, The Hermit, The Wheel of Fortune, Justice, The Hanged Man, Death, Temperance, The Devil, The Tower, The Star, The Moon, The Sun, Judgment, The World.
7. See *Witchcraft, Magic and Alchemy* by Grillot de Givry. Harrap & Co., London, 1931 (page 281).

8. *Histoire de l'haute Magie* by Eliphas Levi. Paris, 1861. Elsewhere in the same volume Levi writes of the Tarot: 'as an erudite Kabalistic book, all combinations of which reveal the harmonies pre-existing between signs, letters, and numbers, the practical value of the Tarot is truly and above all marvellous. A prisoner devoid of books, had he only a Tarot of which he knew how to make use, could in a few years acquire a universal science, and converse with an unequalled doctrine and inexhaustible eloquence.'

9. *The Equinox;* in ten volumes; now a collector's item. The Tarot description is found in Volume VIII.

10. *The Golden Dawn,* by Israel Regardie. Aries Press, Chicago, 1939. In four volumes. Book T is included in Volume IV.

11. Example: In the description of the Ace of Wands, we read: 'The whole is a great and flaming Torch. It symbolizes Force — strength, rush, vigour and energy, and it governs according to its nature, various works and questions'. But, in describing the THREE of PENTACLES, the document says: 'Narrow and prejudiced; cleverness in business, selfishness; keen in matters of gain; sometimes given to seeking after impossibilities'. The contrast in expression is noticeable, the spot card description being undoubtedly applicable to a personality.

   It may be of some interest to readers that every one of the 78 cards in the Tarot pack is attributed, in BOOK T, to some specific part or symbol of the solar system. The 22 keys are divided up between the 12 zodiacal signs, the 7 planets, and the 4 'elements'. The 16 court cards are assigned to definite time periods in the solar year: twelve of them to 30-day periods, and 4 to 90-days periods. The four Aces are allocated, rather vaguely, to the 4 'elements'. The spot cards, as noted, are specifically allied with the 36 ten-degree cycles of the solar year, covering approximately ten calendar days each.

12. Tablet No. 1321 of the Niven collection, described by James Churchward, in *The Children of Mu* (page 41) as 'The Key of the Universe'. Ives Washburn, 1931.

4.

THE WORLD WE LIVE IN

'Science is not just a collection of laws, a catalogue of unrelated facts.
It is a creation of the human mind, with its freely invented ideas and
concepts.'

Albert Einstein

'Perhaps pure science begins where common sense ends.'

Edward Kasner

If the popularization of scientific subjects which has been taking
place during the last few years had accomplished nothing else —
beyond increasing our wonder at the world we live in — it has brought
the scientist and the layman together in a friendly bond of union.
We are losing that feeling of separateness between science and non-
science which prevailed for so long — and which was, after all, only
the natural successor of the superstitious awe with which the average
citizen of the Middle Ages regarded alchemy and magic. As one
modern mathematician puts it: 'For most of the sciences, the veil
of mystery is gradually being torn asunder'. [1]

With this new friendliness from the scientists, the layman is making
the agreeable discovery that the scientists lay no claim to absolute
knowledge about anything. They are not omniscient; they, too, are
still wondering what the terrestrial scheme of things is all about. And
it is notable that many of the scientific writers today are taking an
increasingly lenient view toward the idea that there may have been,
in the far-off past, both science and scientists worthy of the name.
Modern historical research has uncovered evidence that Diodorus,
the 'father of history', was not a creator of fantastics — as had been
believed until recently — but a conscientious and accurate recorder

of events as they actually happened. Mathematicians credit Archimedes with sowing the seed of integral and differential calculus, as we read in *Mathematics and the Imagination* by Kasner and Newman. Physicists are beginning to wonder if changes in the celestial atmosphere are somehow linked with changes in mass psychology; Dr Harlan True Stetson discusses this subject for the layman in *Sunspots and Their Effects From the Human Point of View*. Biologists have begun to consider, and even to study seriously, the ancient and hitherto discredited idea of the possible effects of the season of birth on individual human capacities and energies.

Season of Birth, by Dr Ellsworth Huntingdon of Yale University, was published in 1937. It contains a full report of extensive studies carried out during the twenty years preceding its publication, in the interests of biological research, genetics, and eugenics, directly from the point of view of birthdate-conditioning of individuals and groups. Seasons, rather than shorter periods of the year, form the actual basis of this general research, but months enter into the records, of necessity, which makes possible a broad check of Dr Huntingdon's report of statistical findings against the pattern of the Ten-Day Cycle Formula. The results of this checkup are interesting, as they show several factors which suggest that the scientists of antiquity not only knew their astronomy and mathematics, but their biology as well, and that their system of psychology may have included all three departments of science. It seems, too, that in the language of symbolism — used by the scholars of antiquity to avoid semantic difficulties — there was a racy element of humour.

One of the principal facts set forth in *Season of Birth* is that there is an unmistakable 'peak season' for the birthdates of famous people. This season comes in January, February, and March, of any year, with the peak of the period itself falling around the middle of February. More *famous* people are born during this period than at any other time of the year.

The traditional twelve types of 'astrology' show no correlation with this phenomenon. The zodiacal periods included in the peak period are Capricorn, Aquarius, and Pisces, none of which is credited in the textbooks with the bestowal of either ambition or brilliance as birthday gifts. Capricornians are said to be practical and plodding, Aquarians are supposed to be humanitarians, and Pisceans, the textbooks say, are spiritually-minded, not at all interested in earthly fame.

The Ten-Day Cycle Formula, however, shows an immediate correspondence with the peak of famous births 'discovered' by 20th-century biologists. From the first cycle of January (the THREE of Capricorn) to the turn of the astronomical year in March, the psychological factors suggested by the formula symbols, as well as the characteristics set forth in the original descriptions, and the names given to the corresponding Tarot cards, all show a series of clear pictures of *the kind of people* who are capable of attaining fame and eminence in worldly affairs. The card standing at the peak of the fame cycle — the SIX of Aquarius in the Formula — is entitled '*Earned Success*', and the titles of the cards preceding and following it in the series are equally suggestive of the success idea. The scientists of antiquity were evidently aware of the 'peak of fame' period. And more than this: it is equally evident that the eugenists of ancient Greece and Egypt had arrived at the same conclusion as do our modern experts concerning the cause of the peak.

Dr Huntingdon reported that modern scientists believe the peak of famous births, coming as it does during the first three months of the calendar year, is due to the fact that conceptions of these births take place in the spring, and that the quality of vitality in the springtide conceptions has something to do with the birth of better babies in midwinter. The symbols of the zodiac indicate that the original 'astrologers' were also aware of this.

No one knows who named the constellations, or why. It is probable that when the astronomical pattern, as we know it today, was first recorded, the constellation ARIES actually rose with the Sun at, or close to, the spring point of March 21, the traditional beginning of the New Year. Due to the precession of the equinoxes, of course, the constellations have shifted, and ARIES is no longer the sunrise sign on March 21, as far as constellations are concerned. This, as will be seen, does not affect the formula in any way. ARIES — like everything else in ancient days — was *a symbol only* — representing in this case simply the first 30-degree period of the solar year. It begins to look as if the naming of the zodiacal 'signs' was a subtle and significant gesture on the part of antiquity's astronomer-psychologists, having nothing to do with the actual constellations, but only with the annual sequence of the 30-degree periods.

The first three 'signs' of spring — from March 21 to June 21 — are named, respectively: ARIES, the RAM; TAURUS, the BULL; and GEMINI, commonly called THE TWINS, but originally known as THE LOVERS. In ancient times, as now, the RAM and BULL were symbols of sexual virility, and the LOVERS, as a symbol, speaks for itself. This is a perfect example of the creative, functional use of symbolism as a scientific language.

Thus it seems that the ancient scientists were not unaware of the potentialities of spring as a mating season. They not only named the conception periods with symbolic skill and artistry. They supplied, as well, in the Ten-Day Cycle record, detailed definitions of the resultant characteristics in the psychology of the corresponding birth periods, and named the Tarot cards accordingly. Still another correlation is suggested in the diagram in the end-papers of the book which shows the year as a series of four 'waves', with the peak of famous births coinciding exactly with the peak of the fourth wave.* This fourth wave can be taken, without too great a stretch of the imagination — and present-day authorities say that mathematics implies the use of the imagination — to be the highest point in the four-wave series of the year, like the climax of a four-beat measure in music. Statistics of the Ten-Day Cycle research show an unmistakable peak of famous births at that point in the year. More famous people manage to be born between January 30 and February 9 than in any other single cycle of the year.

The Formula — as frequently seems to happen — goes a step or two beyond the biological statistics. 'Season of birth' leaves us with the uneasy feeling that unless we had the luck to pick a birthday between January and April we might as well apply immediately for admission to the relief rolls. The Ten-Day Cycle Formula gives us at least an even break, no matter when we happen to be born, and it also indicates no less than three other 'peaks of fame' in the birth pattern of the year, all of which have proved accurate under test. Every SIX cycle constitutes one of these peaks, for the simple and logical reason that the potential of SIX is *ambition*. The SIXES are the people who really want to be famous — and a surprisingly large number of them manage to get what they want, as the records show. The statistics on this point would satisfy even a mathematician: out of a casually selected list of 420 outstandingly famous people, 80 were born in one or other of the SIX cycles, and of these 80, no less than 30 were born in the cycle at the peak of the fourth wave, the SIX of Aquarius. It has been found, too, that the less well-known people who are born in any one of the SIX cycles possess a definite type of personal forcefulness and power that is common to all of them. Experimentation with friends — and enemies — as well as with famous names, will show this to be true in the great majority of cases.

It seems possible that one reason why the ancient scientists succeeded in tabulating so accurate and applicable a personality quotient as the Ten-Day Cycle Formula was that they were more interested in people than in atoms, ions, or ergs, and so related their discoveries primarily to man himself. It seems likely, too, that they must have been aware of what Dr Jung called '*the qualities of time*', and which he described thus:

'It seems, indeed, as though time, far from being an abstraction, is a concrete continuum which contains qualities of basic conditions manifesting themselves simultaneously in various places in a way not to be explained by casual parallelisms. The fact that it is possible to construct, in adequate fashion, a person's character from the data of his nativity, shows the relative value of astrology.

'But the birth never depends on the actual astronomical constellations, but on an arbitrary, purely conceptual time-system, because by reason of the precession of the equinoxes, the spring point has long passed on beyond zero degree of Aries. In so far as there are really correct astrological deductions, they are not due to the effect of the constellations, but to our hypothetical time-characters. In other words, whatever is born or done this moment of time *has the qualities of this moment of time.*'[1]

Dr Jung's picture of time as a *concrete continuum* accords very closely with the idea of modern physics that time and space are not two separate things, but one. As Sir James Jeans put it:

'Nature knows nothing of space and time separately, being concerned only with the four-dimensional continuum in which space and time are welded inseparably together into the product we may designate as *spacetime.*'

The human viewpoint, Sir James continued, is necessarily astigmatic when it comes to observing the workings of the universe. But, he added:

'When we take off our human spectacles, we see that an event no longer occurs at a point in space and at an instant of time, but rather exists at a point of the continuum, this point identifying both time and place of the occurrence.'[2]

The accuracy of the Ten-Day Cycle Formula seems to suggest that somebody, sometime, somewhere, took off those human spectacles Sir James spoke of, and succeeded in analyzing *the qualities of time*. How it was done, nobody knows, but its result are much too realistic to allow of indulgence in those alibis of mysticism, intuition, divine inspiration, and the like. It has been suggested already that the only possible way of creating such a record as that of the Ten-Day Cycle Formula would be by the method of statistical research, and that therefore this must have been the method employed in its original construction.[3]

During the last quarter of a century, modern respect for the civilizations of antiquity has been considerably augmented. The beginning of the Christian era is no longer a miraculous turning point, behind which looms a superstitious world, devoid of science, with religions based entirely on mythological fantasies. Especially has the final period of Alexandrian culture — those last amazing centuries before Christ — risen in the estimation of modern scholars.

Historians are agreed that the Alexandrian astronomers knew that the sun was the centre of the planetary system, as Pythagoras had taught several centuries earlier,[4]. and that the earth was round. Archimedes and Euclid were two of the brightest stars of the Alexandrian period; and Eratosthenes, one of the last of the great Librarians, measured the terrestrial circumference with almost perfect accuracy by mathematical calculations.[5] It was not until the second century AD, when Ptolemy pronounced the earth to be the stationary centre of the celestial system, and set himself up as a sort of intellectual dictator, that the truth about the universe was lost, not to be recovered for nearly fifteen centuries. Ptolemy was never popular among the scholars. Hippolytus, in his *Refutation of all Heresies*, wrote passionately: 'O incredible belief, that Ptolemy should be considered preeminently wise among those who have cultivated similar wisdom!'[6] Under Ptolemy's rule the Alexandrian culture, product of the ancient Egyptian, Babylonian, Hebrew, and Grecian civilizations, began to die.

The Ptolemaic theory of a stationary earth was adopted by the early Christian Church, as it accorded so neatly with early Christian beliefs. This fact undoubtedly played a part in ushering in the almost incredible blackout of learning and knowledge — described in the previous chapter — which lasted from the time of Ptolemy, in the 2nd century AD, to the time of Copernicus, who was born in 1473. It will be remembered that the Tarot legend gives the date 1200 AD as the approximate time of the invention of the pack of cards, in which, presumably, certain of the teachings of ancient science were embodied to escape destruction by Christians and barbarians alike.

During the Dark Ages, two subjects in particular were forbidden territory — the heavens, and human destiny. These matters were under the direct authority of the Church. The heavens were set apart as the place where the righteous might arrive after death, and as such had nothing to do with life on earth. Such an idea was pure heresy. Human destiny was determined by God, and God was the province of the Church. Any other theory than this, being unsanctioned by episcopal totalitarianism, caused its perpetrator to be promptly and painfully liquidated. The progress of science, brought to an undeniable height of achievement during the Alexandrian period, was halted. If episcopal authority declared — as it did — that the earth was flat and stationary, while the sun and planets revolved respectfully around it to the glory of God, that settled the matter. There can be little doubt that during the Dark Ages much valuable knowledge was irrevocably lost.

Certain records, however — as previously noted — have remained. And from an unprejudiced study of both ancient and modern statements, it seems that there is a perceptible similarity between the new and old conceptions of the structure of the world we live in.

One of the basic concepts of ancient science was that the universe is constructed, primarily, of ONE substance, which was called, loosely, LIGHT. The scientists of antiquity said that this light was invisible to human eyes, but that its vibrations were in and around everything on earth and in the heavens. They said, too, that it was possible to learn to recognize, understand, and even to use and control this 'light'. Today, modern physics sees the universe — including everything on earth — as being made up of eternally pulsating waves of something, nobody knows what, that is believed to be electrical in nature. With the development of this hypothesis, there has grown up the theory of the *field*, which embraces relativity, the field theory, and the quanta theory. It is in *The Evolution of Physics* — a very readable book on this subject, for the layman — that Einstein said 'to the physicist, the field is as real as the chair on which he sits'. [6]

Physics, as a science, deals with the study of force and energy, motion, temperature, vibration, and such matters, including of course electricity. In non-technical terms, the field of the earth is the *subtle atmosphere* of the world we live in. Radio gave proof of the existence of the field through the discovery of the ionosphere — literally a sphere surrounding the earth with such conformity that its outer shell provides a ceiling against which radio waves bump their heads and bounce back. The science of ionospherics is able to measure the variables of energy within this field, and it has been found that the increase and decrease of energy throughout the solar year is regular, and follows a recurrent pattern. It has also been found that the primary causal factor of the changes is in, or from, the sun itself. [7]

The importance of the sun in the earthly scheme of things is becoming more and more evident with the development of scientific research along these lines. The sun-worshippers of antiquity may have had more reason than superstition in their rituals. From the simple matter of bodily health to the functioning of our most intricate radio apparatus, it seems we are dependent on the sun, whose golden orb was worshipped as a god by the very people who were bright enough to build the Great Pyramid at Giza. Today, the study of solar radiation and its possible effects on the world we live in — and on mankind, both individually and in the mass — is one of the major problems of scientific research. As Dr Stetson, sun-spot expert, put it:

'However fascinating may be the far-off worlds, and however intriguing remote galaxies may appear in our big telescopes, the sun is certainly the most important star to us as human beings living on the planet earth.' [8]

Taking into consideration, then, that the sun is of primary importance to us, and that changes in the field of the earth are evidently traceable to changes in solar radiation — as evidenced by ionospheric research — it is interesting to compare the phrasing of a very ancient scientific statement on the subject with that of a very modern one.

In one of the oldest surviving records of ancient knowledge, called *The Emerald Table of Hermes*, date and author unknown, is found this axiom:

'That which is above is as that which is below, and that which is below is as that which is above . . . This is the strong froce of all forces, overcoming every subtle and penetrating every solid thing. What I have to say is completed *concerning the operation of the Sun.*'

This tablet, which is regarded by historians and scientists as an enigma, and by mystics and occultists as sacred metaphysics, may turn out to be only a clear statement of scientific fact. Place beside it a comment made by Dr Stetson, relating to the sun-spot cycles and their measured effects on earth life:

'With any changes taking place in the electrical charges of the upper air, we should expect to find corresponding changes taking place in the earth's magnetism.' [9]

Some physicist or mathematician of the future will be better able to interpret this striking correlation of ideas than has been done up to the present. But, with the Ten-Day Cycle Formula in our hands as a working hypothesis, it seems that its orderly timing of changing types of energy may have some very close connection with the known changes in solar radiation — not only in the annual pattern which provides the basis of the personality formula, but in those longer time cycles which are the chief producers of headaches among statisticians in the business world and Wall Street.

Simply stated, it seems that the world we live in is an orderly kingdom, with the sun occupying the post of a powerful monarch, whose intentions toward his subjects are entirely constructive, if only they can be understood. We live within the field of the earth, which we now believe to be a product of the sun-earth relationship — that is, of the revolution of the earth around the sun, which has been going on for a considerable period of time without changing its procedure. We respond *physically* to the changing seasons by shedding or adding clothing, by buying ice or coal. Is it impossible to think that we may also respond to the subtle changes in the 'field', which may affect our *psychological* sensibilities just as cold and heat affect our bodies? Only through some such hypothesis as this can the thoroughly practical results of the Ten-Day Cycle Formula be explained.

The ancient concept held that a human being was constructed along the same lines as the universe; that the individual was a sort of replica of the solar system, complete with sun and planets. The Sun symbolized his central powerhouse, or his heart; Venus, his emotions; Mars, his fighting qualities; Mercury, his mind; Jupiter, his sense of justice; Saturn, his sense of discipline and co-ordination.

Modern science — especially since the advent of the field theory — has been coming to the conclusion that man, like everything else in nature, is constructed on electrical principles. Not only does he live within the field of the earth, absorbing its vibrations constantly, he himself is surrounded and enveloped by a perfectly good field of his own corresponding in its essential elements to the earth field, and reacting to the changes in that field. Dr Stetson wrote on this point:

'One thing appears to be certain — that researches in modern medicine and in the nature of electricity and the structure of matter are making us more and more electrically conscious, and, in turn, explaining our very consciousness in terms of electricity.' [10]

It is only by adhering to known scientific laws that new postulates can be formulated. The whole idea of birthdate-conditioning (which has no known laws) can be expressed very simply in terms of biological procedure, linked with the field theory and the idea that 'our very consciousness' can be explained in terms of electricity. If the physical body, in all its ordered complexity, can spring from an infinitesimally tiny nucleus, formed at the moment of conception, why can there not be a psychological nucleus also, which is absorbed from the field at the time of birth?

In other words, would it not be possible that at the moment of time when the individual becomes a part of the earth's field, at birth, with the drawing of the first breath, the newborn organism *receives a charge from that moment of time*, whose qualities create the nucleus of the psychological equipment of the individual?

This is, at least, a question worth considering.

If birthdate-conditioning comes to take its place as a factor in the human scheme of things — and the Formula would seem to suggest that it can do so — our general conception of the human race, as such, will be considerably modified. The apparently unattainable ideal of 'universal brotherhood' takes on a faint semblance of possibility in the light of our growing understanding of each other and of our own individual places in the structure of the human family.

We will not make the mistake, however, of regarding all and sundry as good fellows just because they happen to be human. By means of the Formula we will know, if a Hitler looms on the horizon, that the negative side of any FIVE of Taurus induces an inordinate desire for power, and we will not credit him with virtues and desires that are quite foreign to his nature. Nor will we delegate a flexible TEN of Pisces, like Chamberlain, to meet the hard cunning of a Hitler. What was needed in such a case as the never-to-be-forgotten Munich crisis was a British Mussolini — a FIVE against a FIVE, or some other *dynamic* personality with a positive potential and a powerful frequency. Napoleon, who was a SEVEN of Leo, might have done the job of handling Hitler in that crisis; the picture can be easily imagined!

The very important matter of sending the right man to do the right job can be expedited by the use of the Formula, as has been proved by its practical application during its experimental stages. From this point on, it is not difficult to see how that particular application of the Formula could expand into the development of a general clear-sighted tolerance toward each other on the part of all of us. And this, undeniably, would make the world we live in a much more satisfactory abode, for most of us, than has hitherto been the case.

Notes

1. *Secret of the Golden Flower* by Richard Wilhelm, with commentary by C. G. Jung (page 143). Harcourt Brace, 1931.
2. *The New Background of Science*, Macmillan, 1933 (page 101).
3. *Mathematics for the Million* by Lancelot Hogden, Norton (page 64).
4. In *The Seven Seals of Science* Mayer says: 'The Copernican System was really begun by Pythagoras in ancient times and completed by Kepler in the 16th Century.'
5. See *Ancient Times: A History of the Early World* by J. H. Breasted. (pp. 469-70). Eratosthenes computed the diameter of the earth as being 7850 miles, which is within 50 miles of being correct.

6. *The Evolution of Physics* by Einstein and Infeld. Simon & Schuster, 1938 (page 158).

7. See *Scientific Progress*, Macmillan, 1936, chapter on 'Electricity in the Atmosphere' by Professor E. V. Appleton, F. R. S. (page 74).

8. *Sunspots and Their Effects* by Harlan True Stetson. McGraw-Hill, 1937 (page 10).

9. Same as above (page 134).

10. Same as above (page 137).

* In connection with the diagram of the four waves of the solar year (see pages 8–9) it is interesting to note that modern scientists are discarding the custom of timing the start of the seasons with the equinoctial points and solstice dates. These, it begins to appear, are really the mid-point of the seasons, and not their beginning. It is found that the summer season starts *about May 4* and ends *about August 4*, when autumn really begins. These two dates, falling as they do in the *peak cycles* of the Formula's series of annual waves, suggest a further correlation between the ancient sources of the Formula and the findings of modern physics and astronomy.

5.

THE QUALITIES OF TIME

It will be obvious by now to the readers of this book that if the Ten-Day Cycle Formula functions as described in relation to birthdate-conditioning and individual psychology, it must also have a broader, general application to mass psychology. That is, if the recurrent changes in the earth's field, throughout the solar year, as defined by the Formula, affect the individual at birth to the extent that seems — from the evidence — to be the case, it appears to be probable that these same changes would play a part in the constant shifting of human moods and feelings that we call mass, or crowd psychology. As Dr Jung has put it, it is not only that which is *born* in a moment of time which 'takes on the qualities of that moment of time', but also that which is *done*[1] — actions, events, happenings.

In the early stages of the ten-day cycle research, while the Formula was taking shape, it became more and more evident that logically the response of people in general to what was going on at any given time, in the world, *should* be conditioned by the psychological qualities of the current cycle, so a special study of this question was undertaken. Certain cycles, as can be seen from their analysis, seem to induce certain basic tendencies in individuals, such as optimism, pessimism, peacefulness, combativeness, energy, lethargy, hope, and fear. There are cycles which apparently induce a quality of steady, practical industry; others are indecisive and unstable in nature. By adhering closely to these fundamentals, while following current world events, and checking the observable response of the public as recorded in the news, it was found that with most of the cyclic changes, a corresponding change in public psychology could be detected.

For the proper development of such a research as this promised to be — and it has more than fulfilled its early promise — a lifetime of work would be necessary. Unprejudiced observation of human events and conditions is almost impossible to achieve, and is, of course, necessary to the success of any statistical study. A scientist can watch, through his microscope or in his test tube, changes taking place in the material of his experiments, and make his records with impersonal accuracy. It is much more difficult to judge the changes taking place in the broad waves of human emotion as they are reflected by events; only a robot can be impersonal about wars, revolutions, or elections! It became necessary, therefore, to find some field of human activity to serve as an experimental guinea pig for the study of changing mass psychology in relation to the ten-day cycles. This has to be a field of activity involving many people, and one in which the changes of psychology would have an effect that was definite enough to be recorded in some fashion. If possible, this record should be an official, public record whose data could not be questioned, or give rise to any alibis.

It happened fortunately, that just such a guinea pig presented itself at the right moment. The writer happened to be married to a man whose primary interest in life was the economic principles of finance, and who had been, for many years, a close observer of the fluctuations of the New York Stock Market. It is generally admitted, by the people who are most familiar with this field of activity, that markets move up and down in direct response to psychological impulses — not, as often believed, because of some logical or calculable combination of events or conditions. Of course, in the madhouse known as Wall Street, every second person you encounter has a new theory about what makes the Market move, and if you put your trust in any one of them you are liable to lose your shirt. These things are too well known to call for further comment here; the reference is made only to stress the fact that in adopting the Stock Market as a guinea pig to study the qualities of time and the ten-day cycles, there was no intent to establish a tipster service or to invade the sacred precincts of the investment counsellors.

The point of the whole matter was that the Stock Market fulfilled the two major requirements for such a test. Stock Market prices fluctuate as 'market psychology' shifts from optimism to pessimism, from hope to fear, from confidence to panic. And every day, in the public press, the average price changes are charted and recorded in the form of standard graphs. Thus the Stock Market provides an almost perfect subject for checking the actual response of a very large number, or group, of individuals to the cyclic changes of mass psychology; the average charts tell the story from day to day, and there is little danger of self-deception or illusion.

In the forty-five years since this research was started, many interesting factors have shown themselves. New ground was being broken, from the beginning, as the idea of approaching a study of Stock Market action from the psychological angle only — leaving all other alleged angles of causation strictly alone — was so revolutionary that it was like learning to play a new musical instrument by means of a technique that nobody understood. Very early in the experiment, however, it was found that during ten-day cycles having strongly marked characteristics of optimism or pessimism, the Market was likely to reach the climax of a move up or down, and to change its trend at the end of the cycle in question. It was found that a very large percentage of trend changes take place on a turn from one ten-day cycle to another; during a specially charted period of six years, three out of four trend changes occurred within twenty-four hours of a cycle turn. And, apart from the timing of actual trend changes — which are, of course, vitally interesting to traders and investors — there grew up an increasing amount of evidence that the response of the trading public to current conditions *does* change with the ten-day cycles, even when the most logical thinking can find no reason for the change. Financial writers confess themselves puzzled, most of the time, to account for the vagaries of the trading mood. A volume could be filled with examples of sudden shifts of Market psychology for which no reason could be found, next morning, by the most astute of Stock Market columnists. The great majority of these sudden changes happen at the turn of a ten-day cycle — as can be seen from the study of any standard chart of averages, and from current observation of Stock Market action in relation to the cycles.

The Stock Market, being, as it were, a world of its own within the broader world, and responding in its own particular fashion to the changing forces in the field of the solar year, served as a guide for accuracy in translating the Formula symbols from terms of individual psychology to those of mass psychology. Much was learned through this experiment about the practical value of positive and negative expressions of the cycles, about the interplay of potential and frequency, about the underlying force of the basic quality in every cycle. And out of this work grew also what can only be described as a logical extension of the cycle theory, providing a platform for the calculation of long-range time cycles during which the prevailing mood of the world can be appraised, and a fair judgment arrived at as to when that prevailing mood may be expected to change, and in what general direction. This does not come under the head of prophecy in its usual sense, which is the prediction of events. The use of the Ten-Day Cycle Formula in the judging of changing world trends is concerned only with the changes in psychology — *the way people feel* about what is going on.

The extensive historical research which remains to be done in this field is one of tremendous scope and interest; so far, the surface of the long-range cycle study has hardly been scratched. But enough has been accomplished to show very clearly that there *is* an orderly, definable sequence of changes in the 'qualities of time', and that the Ten-Day Cycle Formula provides a workable starting-point for the measuring of the order and the definition of the changes.

The practical application of the long-range cycles in the study of changing mass psychology is by no means as simple and direct as the correlation of the ten-day cycles with individual characters — the differences between the two processes somewhat resembles the contrast between arithmetic and calculus. The writer makes no claim to have mastered the calculus department of the Formula, but only to have found that it exists, and to have made a beginning, with the co-operation of others, in its development. Here again, the Stock Market provides dependable working evidence, but the implications of the long-range changes in mass psychology of course reach far beyond financial or political phenomena, and touch the deeper instincts of life. This side of the subject, it is hoped, will be developed in a later volume, and it has been introduced here simply to answer the questions that are likely to arise in the mind of the reader as to the possible broader applications of the Ten-Day Cycle Formula.

The idea of time as having qualities, or as a factor of causality in any sense, is of course an unfamiliar one to our present-day thinking. It has not always been so; as noted elsewhere, certain periods of undoubtedly high civilization and culture have accepted the time-causality theory without quibbling and that is why such curiously accurate records as BOOK T, containing the Tarot card descriptions, exist today. Dr Jung, who was noted for his broad-minded approach to such questions as these, named the time-causality hypothesis *the synchronistic principle*, which he described as 'the relative simultaneity of basic conditions manifesting themselves simultaneously in various places in a way not to be explained by causal parallelisms.' [2]

As Dr Jung pointed out, this type of thinking has been missing from the philosophical structure of the world since the time of Heraclitus, but has never been completely lost. It has taken, as is well known, some strange and unconvincing forms, in the hands of charlatans and soothsayers. The Ten-Day Formula, being a clear and simple pattern of the solar year in terms of everyday psychology, need not be classed with the twilight speculations of the fortunetelling fraternity. It approaches, rather, the field, or the space-time continuum of modern physics, which even the physicists do not claim to understand. Einstein wrote of it:

'A new concept appears in physics, the most important invention since Newton's time: the field. It needed great scientific imagination to realize that it is not the charges nor the particles but the field in the space between the charges and the particles which is essential for the description of physical phenomena. The field concept proves most successful and leads to the formulation of Maxwell's equations describing the structure of the electromagnetic field and governing the electric as well as the optical phenomena.

'The theory of relativity arises from the field problems. The contradictions and inconsistencies of the old theories force us to ascribe new properties to the time-space continuum, to the scene of all events in our physical world.' [3]

Out of the mouths of babes, we are told, comes wisdom. It may be that out of the study of Stock Market action and the Ten-Day Cycle Formula can come at least a few of the answers to the scientific problem of the time-space continuum, as well as to the eternal problem of why people behave the way they do.

Notes

1. *The Secret of the Golden Flower* by Wilhelm, with commentary by Dr Jung. A lengthy commentary by Dr Jung on the subject of time-conditioning is found in the final section of the book, beginning on page 143. Harcourt Brace, New York.
2. See Note 1.
3. *Evolution of Physics* by Einstein and Infeld. Simon & Schuster, 1938 (page 259). The whole of the section of this interesting book under the heading of 'Field, Relativity', is of definite interest in relation to the ten-day cycle research and will repay a survey by the reader.

6.

PURSUIT OF DESTINY

Like many other words, through careless use, the word *destiny* has gained an undeserved opprobrium. It has been given a fatalistic meaning quite foreign to its true Latin root, which is much more clearly expressed in another of its derivatives, the word *destination*. In the title of this book, and the heading of this chapter, destiny is used in the sense of being a goal — a destination — chosen and pursued by the individual entirely according to his own free will. There is nothing fatalistic, unavoidable, or inevitable about anyone's destiny according to the Ten-Day Cycle Formula.

The thought of being classified, labelled, or ticketed like a bargain counter item has always been repugnant to evolving mankind. This repugnance is probably one of the factors which has prevented the ancient theories of birthdate-conditioning from receiving adequate attention and analysis from modern science; those theories which, because of their dubious forms of presentation, have seemed to be both absurd and insulting to human intelligence. The same objection, in the main, applies to the many different attempts made by psychologists and biologists to divide the human family arbitrarily into groups according to symptoms displayed in behaviour, appearance, or reactions. We simply do not like the idea of being told precisely what we are, or are not — and yet so contrary is human nature that many of us are constantly searching the bypaths of learning for this or that answer to the problems of self-knowledge and self-understanding. Any catalogue of cultist literature gives evidence of this; any astute charlatan can make a successful racket of a secret method of personality analysis. It is a popular subject, one might say, for private consumption only. Admitting publicly to any classification, however, is something else again; we do not like it.

It is for this apparently contradictory reason that the Ten-Day Cycle Formula has been condensed, however inadequately, between the covers of this book. Anyone, observing the world today, or through the hindsight of history, cannot help being conscious of the tremendous hunger of human individuals for a place in the scheme of things to which they have an inalienable right. This hunger takes a thousand different forms; it lies at the root of practically every endeavour, either good or evil, constructive or destructive, by individuals, groups, or nations. And it is to be noted that whenever a certain measure of this hunger is satisfied by the achievement of what we call *freedom*, the best things are accomplished — either by the individual, the group, or the nation.

In the case of the individual — with whom this work is most directly concerned — such a sense of freedom can only come from natural self-respect. It is hard to respect anything that we feel to be inadequate — and a large majority of us, as noted earlier, suffer from a feeling of inadequacy forced upon us by artificial standards of personal judgment. Here, it seems, the Ten-Day Cycle Formula makes its most valuable contribution, without annoying or insulting us by arbitrary classification. It shows us a *natural* pattern of humanity, into which we fit, as individuals, by the inalienable right of birth. And, without limiting our possibilities for achievement, attainment, or happiness in any way, it suggests the natural line of least resistance for each one of us to take in the pursuit of destiny — natural, because it is our own; something that nobody can ever take away from us.

Always, in trying to evaluate or to sum up the fundamentals of the Formula — after working with it for so many years — the writer feels rather like the poet who tried for weeks to write a description of a particularly beautiful sunset, and ended by producing two lines in iambic pentameter:

> 'Beauty, whose wordlessness has stilled my pen,
> Cannot be told, but must be seen by men.'

Because of the infinite variety of human response, it is only presumptuous to try, in any way, to anticipate the reactions of an individual reader to the facts and theories, modern and ancient, that comprise the Formula. In other words, the poet can never describe the sunset; you have to see it with your own eyes. This picture of the solar year, with its recurrent series of orderly cycles, depending for their changes on the relationship between the earth and sun — which has never changed — will carry its own meaning to you who read about it. The conception of the field of the earth, changing regularly in potential, frequency, and quality, to which we must respond, each in his own way, because we live within it, will take its own form in your mental vision.

It has been found, however, that one of the most constructive suggestions arising from the Formula is this very idea of *change*. People who are optimistic by nature will find it easy to believe that a mood of black despair will pass — that 'we'll feel better about it all' next week, or next month. But for those of us who lack the adaptability of natural optimism, and must depend upon our reason or logic, it is comforting to know that within a short time the cloud of gloom under which we seem to be buried today will transmute itself into something else quite different — hope, determination, or simply equilibrium — in response to the changes in the qualities of time. This really happens, though it is hard to believe until we have begun to observe it.

For instance, in the spring of 1940, the world was plunged into panic on the tenth of May by the sudden invasion of Holland and Belgium by Hitler. The eleventh of May is the first day of the SEVEN of Taurus cycle, which on its negative side exhibits a pessimistic and cowardly field of force which has a tendency to dominate over the positive factors. The panic which began on the eleventh of May was astonishing in its proportions. Even the sanest of radio commentators flooded the air with hopelessness, and the headlines grew daily more alarming. Stock markets sold off violently — until the twenty-first of May, when with the change of cycle and abrupt shift from panic to confidence, from fear to courage, from despair to determination, took place. The commentators took heart; the headlines brightened; in London and New York the markets turned up. *Nothing had happened to cause this change*; the situation in Europe was appalling. But the spirit of the world — led, as it happened, by England — changed almost overnight from one of negative cowardice to one of positive confidence, in response to the stability and strength of the

EIGHT of Gemini cycle. This is only one example of many that have been observed and recorded during the course of the ten-day cycle research, and it is cited as an illustration of the value of the cycle theory in the matter of retaining equilibrium during periods of panic — and still more, of retaining that confidence in the future without which life would be rather a sad affair at best.

Confidence in the future, confidence in ourselves, and tolerance for other people, bred of understanding — these things the Formula offers us, whether we accept them or reject them. It is perhaps significant that its appearance at this time should coincide with what seems, to the hopeful observer, to be a general return on the part of humanity to the ideals of individualism. Not the rugged individualism which tramples on the weak to reach its goal, but the true individualism of the self-respecting man and woman, which pursues its destiny in its own way, according to its own desires, and grants a like freedom to other individuals. This is not a philosophy of selfishness; the true desire of a self-respecting individual is never one that will bring hurt or harm to others, and the self-respecting individual keeps to the basic standards of honesty and decency without which there can be no self-respect.

Destiny, in the light of the pattern of time bequeathed to us by unknown benefactors of the past, becomes, like the *Tao* of Chinese philosophy, both the road we travel on and the goal toward which we are heading. We are comfortably conscious of being part of an orderly structure of life, but fully aware at the same time that we are free to choose for ourselves what use we will make of the weapons furnished to us as our birthright. But the Formula assures us, with uncompromising frankness, that destiny is not something handed to us by a benevolent — or malevolent — fate. We are given certain weapons out of the orderly arsenal of nature; their use is up to us. Destiny is something to be achieved, to be fought for, to be pursued. This, probably, is why the Ten-Day Cycle pattern of time and birthdate-conditioning resolved itself, as it developed, into a formula — a formula for the pursuit of destiny.